PERSONAL FINANCE LIBRARY

INVESTMENT STRATEGIES

HOW TO CREATE

YOUR OWN & MAKE IT

WORK FOR YOU

BY SEYMOUR FRIEDLAND & STEVEN G. KELMAN

Canadian Cataloguing in Publication Data

Kelman, Steven G. (Steven Gershon), 1945
        Investment Strategies
(Personal finance library) Canadian ed.
Earlier ed. published under title: What you should know about your personal finances.

ISBN 0-14-010606-5

1. Finance, Personal.   2. Investment - Canada.
I. Friedland, Seymour, 1928   II. Title.
III. Title: What you should know about your personal finances.   IV. Series.

HG179.K44 1988   332.024   C88-095024-2

Printed and bound in Canada

CONTENTS

INTRODUCTION

ONLY A FRACTION OF CANADIANS – 10% TO 20%, DEPENDING ON WHOSE estimates you believe – invest in anything other than the guaranteed investments offered by banks, trust companies and other institutions. By excluding alternatives such as bonds, stocks and mutual funds, most investors deprive themselves of significant opportunities for increasing their financial returns. Indeed, many people fail to realize that even small differences in rates of return mean huge differences in results over time. For example, $1,000 a year invested for 25 years at 8% brings in almost $79,000. At 10%, you end up with $108,000; with 12%, $149,000; and with 14%, $207,000.

The purpose of this book is to make you aware of your investment alternatives and how they work. It won't show you how to get rich overnight, but it will show you how to accumulate wealth by using the investment alternatives available to Canadians. It will also demonstrate how other investors have increased their wealth by putting money into varied investment vehicles and, just as important, will help you avoid the pitfalls that have prevented many people from meeting their financial goals. Even if you've already given some thought to financial planning, this book can be a valuable aid. Recent changes in the areas of investment and taxation have made it necessary to review your goals and financial planning strategies.

Perhaps the most significant changes have come as a result of federal tax reforms introduced in 1988. The new rules affect all investors, from those with a few dollars in Canada Savings Bonds who lose out because of elimination of the $1,000 investment-income deduction to high-income earners whose tax rates on capital gains increase dramatically. Tax reform has also ended some tax shelters, although there are still ways for investors to shield income from taxes.

The good news is that Ottawa is finally getting around to reforming pension legislation and the rules regarding registered retirement savings plans (RRSPs). Employees who are members of pension plans will soon have their employer's contributions vested, or locked in on their behalf, after two years. Traditionally, many plans haven't allowed vesting until five or even 10 years, so an employee who leaves a job before that time gets only his or her contributions, and not the company's. In addition, new rules will make pension plans portable, so someone who leaves a company will be able to take his or her pension along, transferring it to the new employer's pension plan or to an RRSP.

About the authors

Born in the United States, Seymour Friedland took his doctorate at Harvard University and came to Canada as Professor of Finance and Economics at York University's Faculty of Administrative Studies, a position he still holds. His 37-year teaching career includes terms at New York University, Claremont Graduate School, Rutgers State University, the Massachusetts Institute of Technology and Harvard.

He has published nine books and numerous articles in academic journals and has served as a consultant to many U.S. and Canadian companies, as well as governments. In addition, he was chief economist for Dominion Securities Ltd. from 1969 to 1974 and for many years Associate Editor of Financial Times. He often appears as a business and economics commentator on television and radio and was Business Editor of CBC Television's The Journal. He won a National Business Writing Award in 1980.

Mr. Friedland now writes a widely syndicated column for Financial Times News Service.

Steven G. Kelman is an investment counsellor and vice-president of Dynamic Capital Corporation, one of Canada's foremost financial service organizations.

He began his association with Financial Times as a staff writer in 1975, becoming Investment Editor in 1977. He is now a Contributing Editor and, as a recognized expert on Canadian mutual funds, is responsible for the Financial Times Monthly Survey of Investment Funds and is editor of Financial Times Mutual Fund Sourcebook. As well, Mr. Kelman is author of RRSPs 1989 and co-author of Understanding Mutual Funds. Both books are part of the Financial Times Personal Finance Library.

He is a Chartered Financial Analyst and a member of the Toronto Society of Financial Analysts. He has also lectured at York University's Faculty of Administrative Studies.

After obtaining his MBA from York University in 1969, Mr. Kelman worked as an analyst and portfolio manager for a major insurance company before becoming a senior analyst with a stock brokerage house. He joined the Dynamic Group of Companies in 1985.

About the editor

David Toole, Financial Times Personal Finance Library Editor, is a Toronto-based freelance writer and editor who specializes in business and personal finance. His journalism experience spans 15 years and includes senior editorial positions with Financial Times of Canada, The Toronto Star and several other major Canadian publications.

Acknowledgements

There are many individuals whose help was essential in publishing this book. We would like to thank Leslie Murray of Dynamic Capital Corporation who kept our files in order; Richard Anstett who provided his insight into market cycles; Financial Times Personal Finance Library Editor David Toole; and Rudy Luukko, Nadine Kostiuk and David Groskind of Financial Times. In particular we would like to thank Ron Blunn, Business Development Manager of the Times, who was responsible for producing Investment Strategies. Thanks also to our colleagues, families and friends for their support during this project.

And finally, we would like to thank David Tafler, Publisher of the Times, for making this book possible.

CHAPTER ONE

HOW TO MAKE A MILLION: SAVE

IT IS STILL ABSURDLY EASY TO BECOME A MILLIONAIRE. JUST FOLLOW the "Rule of 72." The "Rule of 72" is a shorthand way of solving many compound interest problems. When interest is compounded, the amount ultimately recovered from an investment reflects not only the interest earned on the principal, but also the interest earned on interest already paid.

Suppose $1,000 has been invested at 10%, compounded annually. In the first year, interest earnings are $100 (10% of $1,000). If the first year's interest remains invested, the principal in the second year becomes $1,100, and the second year's interest earnings are $110. In the third year, the principal becomes $1,210, and interest earnings are $121. As long as the interest is not withdrawn, compound interest generates an ascending curve of interest earnings.

At the end of five years, the investment will have grown to $1,610.51. With simple interest – where interest is not earned on past interest – the value of the $1,000 at 10% in five years would be only $1,500.

If the investment permitted semi-annual compounding, rather than just annual compounding, interest in the second six months of the first year would include interest on the first half-year's earnings. With semi-annual compounding, the value of the $1,000 at 10% would be worth $1,628.89 after five years, an increase of $18.38 over annual compounding and $128.89 better than simple interest. It follows that quarterly compounding is better still, and monthly compounding better yet.

The effects of compound interest can be quickly calculated by using the Rule of 72. The rule states that the length of time necessary before a compounding investment doubles in value can be determined simply by dividing 72 by the annual interest rate. So the $1,000 invested at 10% will

Table I

How an investment of $1,000 a year can grow over time at different rates of return

Years	8%	10%	12%	14%	16%	18%
1	1,080	1,100	1,120	1,140	1,160	1,180
2	2,246	2,310	2,374	2,440	2,506	2,572
3	3,506	3,641	3,779	3,921	4,066	4,215
4	4,867	5,105	5,353	5,610	5,877	6,154
5	6,336	6,716	7,115	7,536	7,977	8,442
6	7,923	8,487	9,089	9,730	10,414	11,142
7	9,637	10,436	11,300	12,233	13,240	14,327
8	11,488	12,579	13,776	15,085	16,519	18,086
9	13,487	14,937	16,549	18,337	20,321	22,521
10	15,645	17,531	19,655	22,045	24,733	27,755
11	17,977	20,384	23,133	26,271	29,850	33,931
12	20,495	23,523	27,029	31,089	35,786	41,219
13	23,215	26,975	31,393	36,581	42,672	49,818
14	26,152	30,772	36,280	42,842	50,660	59,965
15	29,324	34,950	41,753	49,980	59,925	71,939
16	32,750	39,545	47,884	58,118	70,673	86,068
17	36,450	44,599	54,750	67,394	83,141	102,740
18	40,446	50,159	62,440	77,969	97,603	122,414
19	44,762	56,275	71,052	90,025	114,380	145,628
20	49,423	63,002	80,699	103,768	133,841	173,021

double in value in 7.2 years. If the interest rate had been only 5%, it would take 14.4 years to grow to $2,000. On the other hand, doubling of the original would take place in just 4.8 years at a 15% interest rate.

To find the interest rate that would double your investment in a given number of years, divide 72 by the number of years. For example, to double an investment in six years, one must earn 12%. Another example: the population around the Great Lakes is expected to double in the next 40 years. Using the Rule of 72 – dividing 72 by 40 – the annual population growth is expected to be 1.8%.

Of course, this handy simplification is only an approximation. In reality it would take 7.273 years, not 7.2, to double $1,000 at 10% compounded annually. If the compounding period is shorter, the Rule of 72 overstates the length of time needed to double your investment. Compounded monthly, it takes only 6.96 years for $1,000 to double at 10%.

Table II

The future value of a single deposit of $1,000 using different rates of return

Years	8%	10%	12%	14%	16%	18%
1	1,080	1,100	1,120	1,140	1,160	1,180
2	1,166	1,210	1,254	1,300	1,346	1,392
3	1,260	1,331	1,405	1,482	1,561	1,643
4	1,360	1,464	1,574	1,689	1,811	1,939
5	1,469	1,611	1,762	1,925	2,100	2,288
6	1,587	1,772	1,974	2,195	2,436	2,700
7	1,714	1,949	2,211	2,502	2,826	3,185
8	1,851	2,144	2,476	2,853	3,278	3,759
9	1,999	2,358	2,773	3,252	3,803	4,435
10	2,159	2,594	3,106	3,707	4,411	5,234
11	2,332	2,853	3,479	4,226	5,117	6,176
12	2,518	3,138	3,896	4,818	5,936	7,288
13	2,720	3,452	4,363	5,492	6,886	8,599
14	2,937	3,797	4,887	6,261	7,988	10,147
15	3,172	4,177	5,474	7,138	9,266	11,974
16	3,426	4,595	6,130	8,137	10,748	14,129
17	3,700	5,054	6,866	9,276	12,468	16,672
18	3,996	5,560	7,690	10,575	14,463	19,673
19	4,316	6,116	8,613	12,056	16,777	23,214
20	4,661	6,727	9,646	13,743	19,461	27,393

The real key to making a million

The magic of compounding is much stronger when applied to systematic savings, rather than to a single deposit.

Even at a savings rate of as low as 8% compounded monthly, a 32-year-old can be a millionaire at age 65 simply by saving $500 a month. Back when savings rates were in the 13% to 14% range, hitting the millionaire class would have taken 10 years less. But when rates were about 6%, it would have taken seven years longer.

Table I on page 2 shows the importance of time and rates of return in reaching your goal by demonstrating how annual investments of $1,000 grow over different time periods and at different rates of return. (A more comprehensive table appears in Appendix A.)

Table II shows how a single investment will grow over time at differing rates of return. (A more comprehensive table appears in Appendix B.)

Regardless of the interest rate, the real issue is whether you can raise the needed $500 each month. And that is also the key to successfully using the strategies outlined in this book. Although there are investment ideas discussed in the following chapters that have generated returns far higher than 8%, most require that you contribute some money.

Initial equity in an investment can come from only two sources. The fortunate few may inherit the money, but the rest of us have to do it the old-fashioned way: we must earn it and save it. For most of us, then, becoming rich is merely a dream if we cannot save. And the key to saving is controlling expenditures.

Many savers have found that a budget is essential to control spending. That's why an examination of how the typical Canadian household spends money is a useful starting point in developing that all-important budget.

The three big categories of expenditure are food, shelter and transportation. Depending on where you live – for instance, it costs a lot less for housing in St. John's than in Vancouver – these three items can consume as much as half of the pre-tax income of typical Canadians.

As earnings increase, these basic expenditures account for a lesser percentage of income. The family with an income of $50,000 or more is likely to spend a lesser proportion on food, shelter and transportation than the family with $20,000 of income. And the family with $100,000 will spend an even smaller percentage.

Credit hurts saving

Clearly, savings prospects are improved if you avoid extravagances. And if you avoid extravagant spending, you may also avoid another costly drain on the budget: interest payments on consumer debt.

More than $66 billion of consumer debt (excluding mortgages) is owed by Canadians. Some is owed for money used to purchase automobiles, and a growing portion relates to credit card purchases.

Still, there are times when it is necessary to borrow. If the borrowing is for a business purpose, such as investing in securities, some or all of the interest may be deductible for income tax purposes. If interest is deductible, a 12% interest rate shrinks to as little as 7.2% for a person whose top marginal tax rate is 39%. But without the tax deduction, interest on consumer debt can be a heavy burden, particularly as the interest on an unpaid balance is compounded. That's when compounding turns vicious.

For example, your credit card may charge something like 0.05094% daily on unpaid balances. If that's the case, you are paying an annual in-

Table III
Family Budget Form

Annual Budget	Earner #1	Earner #2	Earner #3
INCOME			
Employment income			
Interest income			
Dividends			
Pension income			
Rental income			
Business income			
Other income			
TOTAL INCOME			
EXPENSES			
Taxes on income			
Mortgage/rent/ utilities/property taxes			
Home maintenance/ furniture			
Transportation/Car			
Food			
Clothing			
Dental/Medical			
Household Contributions			
Loan payments			
Education			
Life and disability insurance			
Entertainment			
Charitable Donations			
TOTAL EXPENSES			
Difference available for savings			
RRSP/Pension contributions			
Other investments			

terest rate of 20.43%. On a balance of $1,000, that means interest costs will exceed the original balance in three years and nine months.

It is much cheaper to go to a bank, trust company or credit union and borrow to pay off your credit card balance – as long as the personal loan rate is less than your card rate. It is cheaper still to operate on a tight budget and owe nothing for transactions that are purely for personal consumption. At today's interest rates, it is far better to be a lender than a borrower.

So the first thing you should do is formulate a budget using the form in Table III on page 5, if only to determine how you are currently spending your money. If you aren't saving anything now, set a target of 10%, then look for areas where you can cut spending to allow for those savings. Your pay slip will show you what you pay in taxes each pay period and your cheque records will provide information about where your money goes. You should also keep track of where your pocket money is spent. Use Table IV on page 7 to track your family earnings and expenditures. And don't forget to include everyone in the family on both the income and expenditure sides. High-income families usually have more income earners than do low-income families.

Setting money aside each month is the first step toward becoming a millionaire. You must institute spending limits that will shave a percentage point or two from those categories that can bear the cut.

Don't give up easily. Food costs, for example, can be cut by anywhere from 10% to 40% by seeking out sales, buying generic products and shopping at food stores that sell out of shipping cartons and have you pack your own groceries. It may cause some inconvenience, but becoming a millionaire requires savings – and that is not painless. But those nickels and dimes you can save will add up. Remember, $10 a week is more than $500 a year. And $500 a year invested at 12% for 25 years is almost $75,000. That's a far cry from a million, but it's a start.

You're wealthier than you think

Admittedly, preparing a budget is almost as painful as holding to budgeted spending limits. But measuring wealth, particularly if it is your own, is a most gratifying experience. It is also a very useful exercise.

Most of us are wealthier than we think. Yet we rarely look at our asset holdings as an investment portfolio, and so we don't try to maximize gains in overall portfolio value. Furthermore, we too often hold a bag of undiversified assets – a risky practice. While diversification is more difficult for individuals than for professional investment managers, the results can be as rewarding.

Table IV

Your balance sheet

ASSETS	Earner #1	Earner #2
Bank accounts		
Canada Savings Bonds		
Other cash investments		
GICs		
Bonds		
Mortgage investments		
Annuities/RRIFs		
Pensions/RRSPs		
Stocks		
Mutual Funds		
Other investments (use market values)		
Cash value of life insurance		
Collectibles		
Furniture		
Cars		
House		
Cottage		
TOTAL ASSETS		
LIABILITIES		
Mortgages		
Bank loans		
Credit cards		
Investment loans		
Other debt		
Total Liabilities		
NET WORTH		

To assess your wealth, you need to determine your net worth. You can do this by adding up the value of everything you own and subtracting everything you owe from that figure. But it isn't really that simple; you have to make some adjustments. For instance, you may think your furniture is worth a great deal, and in fact your house insurance should be based on its replacement value. But for net worth purposes, it should be given a value of $1. In addition, your RRSP may be worth $50,000, but you have to pay tax on that amount when you withdraw. So its true value may be as little as $33,000. Table IV on page 7, can be used as a sample for constructing your personal balance sheet. Don't be shy about adjusting it to suit your circumstances.

If you are a homeowner, your house is probably your biggest asset, although if you recently purchased a house your assets may only slightly exceed your liabilities.

Two of the trickier items to estimate on your balance sheet are life insurance and pensions. Term insurance can be ignored because it has no savings component, but the cash surrender value of whole life insurance should be included. Estimating the value of pensions is also a problem, although this is made easier if your employer sends you pension investment information. Such information usually includes the present value of your pension, which is the amount to include on your personal balance sheet. It is quite difficult to estimate the value of some government retirement program payments because benefits are partly indexed to the cost of living and are subject to unforeseen legislative changes. Ottawa does, however, provide a statement on Canada Pension Plan benefits.

The value of savings in RRSPs is easier to determine. For your balance sheet, include the current value, which is indicated on the statements sent to you by the financial institution holding your funds.

Once you've compiled a list of your assets, consider whether they are diversified enough. The older the head of the household, the more diversified the portfolio should be. Insufficient diversification means putting too many of your eggs in one basket – a pitfall for older people, who have less time to recover from financial disasters that might result when an investment goes sour.

To introduce an element of diversification into a portfolio, it may be necessary to borrow against other assets. Typically, an undiversified personal balance sheet will consist mainly of pension claims and a house with a small mortgage, or with no mortgage at all.

Borrowing against equity in the home, and using the proceeds to buy financial assets such as stocks and bonds, does more than just increase diversification. It allows the interest expense on the loan to be used as a deduction for income tax purposes. Furthermore, interest and dividends using certain investment vehicles offer significant tax benefits.

Home mortgages are the largest single liability for most Canadians. In fact, we have more than $100 billion in outstanding residential mortgages. Moreover, it is a huge pile of debt that is extremely expensive because mortgage interest is not deductible when computing tax liabilities. If you are in the 39% marginal tax bracket and are paying $5,000 annually in mortgage interest, you must earn $8,197 in pre-tax income to cover your after-tax mortgage interest. Those in the 45% tax bracket must earn $9,090.

If you can reduce your mortgage by rapid amortization or by taking advantage of the annual pay-down feature most institutions offer, you save a bundle. Take, for example, the 39%-bracket homeowner who has $10,000 in savings beyond "rainy-day" needs. Earning even 10% before taxes on the savings is not as attractive as using the money to reduce the mortgage. That's because the 10% savings rate is reduced to 6.1% after taxes — a lot less than the 12% after taxes being paid on the mortgage.

For higher-bracket earners, the results are even worse. That 10% before-tax savings rate is only 5.5% after taxes for someone paying a marginal tax rate of 45%. He would be far better off using the savings to pay off the mortgage, which might cost about 10% after taxes. For these high-bracket earners, a risk-free rate of almost 19% would be necessary to break even on an after-tax basis with a 10% mortgage rate.

Most Canadians are well aware of the horrendous mortgage costs they face, and attempt to reduce or eliminate the mortgage as soon as possible. For financial well-being, there's no finer aroma than the smell of a paid-up mortgage being burned to a crisp.

So formulate a balance sheet to tally your worth. (We'll have more to say on your balance sheet later.) After you have completed your balance sheet, review it with the aim of increasing returns and achieving diversification. Then prepare a target balance sheet, setting short- and long-term targets, which you should review each year.

The remaining chapters of the book cover taxation of income, methods of putting your financial house in order, the setting of your investment objectives and your range of investment options. The information in these chapters should be used as tools to help you build your investment program.

But there are other tools you must use, the most important of which is information. As an investor who wants to make the highest returns possible with due concern for risk, you must have a fundamental knowledge of events that have an impact on investment.

CHAPTER TWO

A FINANCIAL TOOLKIT

MOST PROFESSIONAL INVESTORS IN CANADA MAKE A POINT OF READING the business press to keep them informed of general developments in the economy, specific industries and individual companies. Basic reading material includes the Globe and Mail Report on Business, possibly the Wall Street Journal, and a Canadian business weekly such as Financial Times of Canada or The Financial Post. In addition there are numerous specialty publications covering the spectrum of investment alternatives.

But you have to learn to walk before you run. So start with a paper that contains financial tables covering the investment areas that interest you, as well as information on general developments and business trends. Start slowly and expand your reading as your understanding increases. Don't run out and buy subscriptions to every business publication available; most will end up unread.

For example, the papers you choose should keep you informed about interest rate trends and indicate the current rates available. The interest rate trends table, taken from Financial Times of Canada, includes several key short-term interest rates as shown at the top of the next page. The 91-day treasury bill rate indicates what the federal government is paying for short-term money. The yields on treasury bills (T-bills) are adjusted by the Bank of Canada to reflect its policies toward economic growth and the level at which it wishes to maintain the dollar.

All short-term rates, including the rate that banks pay on savings accounts, are based on T-bill yields. The Bank of Canada rate is the rate at which certain deposit-taking institutions can borrow funds from the Bank of Canada. But the key yield, as far as individual investors are concerned, is the T-bill rate.

Trends

Week to Sep. 15	THIS WEEK	LAST WEEK	CHANGE ON WEEK	YEAR AGO	CHANGE ON YEAR
Canada					
Treasury bills (91 days)	10 32	10 10	0 22	9 19	1 13
Commercial paper (90 days)	10 70	10 30	0 40	9 30	1 40
Bankers acceptance (90 days)	10 60	10 25	0 35	9 25	1 35
Banks prime rate	11 75	11 25	0 50	10 00	1 75
Bank of Canada rate	10 57	10 35	0 22	9 44	1 13
Mortgages (trust companies 5 yr conventional rate)	12 00	12 25	-0 25	11 75	0 25
United States					
Treasury bills (91 days)	7 39	7 54	-0 15	6 57	0 82
Commercial paper (90 days)	8 35	8 40	-0 05	7 55	0 80
Banks prime rate	10 00	10 00	0 00	8 75	1 25
Federal reserve discount rate	6 50	6 50	0 00	6 00	0 50
Federal reserve funds rate	8 25	8 13	0 12	7 00	1 25
International					
Eurodollar CD (Secondary) (90 days)	8 25	8 38	-0 13	7 63	0 62

Short-Term Wholesale Rates

Prepared by Fiscal Agents as of September 15, 1988.

CHARTERED BANKS	Minimum Deposit	30 Days	60 Days	90 Days
Canadian Western Bank	100,000	9 30	9 40	9 50
National Bank	100,000	7 75	7 75	7 75
National Bank	250,000	8 00	8 00	8 00

CANADIAN CHARTERED FOREIGN-OWNED BANKS	Minimum Deposit	30 Days	60 Days	90 Days
A.B.N. Bank	100,000	9 62	9 75	9 87
Banca Commerciale Italiana	100,000	9 85	9 95	10 05
Banco Central	100,000	9 35	9 50	9 65
Bank Leumi-Le Israel	100,000	9 87	10 00	10 12
Bank of Credit & Commerce	100,000	8 50	8 56	8 75
Barclays Bank	100,000	9 25	9 25	9 25
Credit Suisse	100,000	9 65	9 75	9 85
Dresdner Bank	100,000	8 75	9 00	9 12
First Chicago	100,000	9 80	9 85	9 90
Hongkong Bank	100,000	8 60	8 75	9 00
Lloyds Bank	100,000	9 20	9 40	9 55
Natwest Canada	50,000	9 25	9 35	9 50
Security Pacific	100,000	9 00	9 00	9 00
Standard Chartered	100,000	9 15	9 15	9 15
Swiss Bank	100,000	9 30	9 50	9 55
Union Bank of Switzerland	100,000	8 50	8 60	8 75

FINANCE, ACCEPTANCE COMPANIES	Minimum Deposit	30-59 Days	60-89 Days	90-119 Days
Ford Credit Canada Ltd.	50,000	10 30	10 35	10 45
G.M.A.C.	50,000	10 38	10 58	10 77
Hudson Bay Finance	100,000	9 50	9 70	9 85

COMMERCIAL PAPER	Minimum Deposit	30 Days	60 Days	90 Days
Caisse Centrale	100,000	10 25	10 35	10 55
E.D.C.	100,000	9 85		
Gendis	100,000	10 35		
Gulf Enterprise	100,000	10 30		
Noranda Mines	100,000	10 35	10 55	10 75
Provigo	100,000	10 40		
S.B.D.B.	100,000	10 05		
Trizec	100,000	10 32		

GOVERNMENT T-BILLS	Minimum Deposit	91 Days	182 Days
Alberta	25,000	10 39	
British Columbia	1,000	10 35	
Canada	1,000	10 32	10 58
Manitoba	25,000	10 22	
New Brunswick	25,000	10 44	
Newfoundland	100,000	10 38	

The next table includes short-term wholesale rates – the interest rates that banks, trust companies, governments and some companies are willing to pay for large amounts of money – usually at least $100,000. The rates shown vary widely, although most are clustered closely together. An institution offering a much lower rate than its competitors is probably indicating that it isn't in need of short-term funds at the time.

The table at the top of the next page shows the rates banks and trust companies are willing to pay for minimum deposits, generally of at least $5,000 and for terms ranging from three months to five years. Interest rates quoted by an institution can change at any time, depending on deposit levels. In fact, rates quoted by an institution on large amounts can change hourly to reflect marketplace trends.

It's also a good idea to keep an eye on bond yields so you can see what governments are paying for medium- and long-term funds. Trends in these areas have a significant impact on mortgage rates and on insurance company annuity rates.

If you invest, or plan to invest, in the stock market you will require a publication containing stock tables. Someone trading daily would almost

Retail Rates

INSTITUTIONS		SHORT					MEDIUM			
								Interest paid annually		
	Minimum	30-59	60-89	90-119	120-179	Minimum				
CHARTERED BANKS	Deposit	Days	Days	Days	Days	Deposit	1 year	3 yrs.	5 yrs.	
Bank of B.C.	5,000	7 25	7 25	7 25	7 50	1,000	10 00	10 25	10 75	
Bank of Montreal	5,000	7 00	7 00	7 00	7 00	1,000	10 00	10 25	10 75	
Bank of Nova Scotia	5,000	7 00	7 00	7 00	7 00	1,000	10 00	10 25	10 75	
Canadian Imperial Bank of Commerce	5,000	7 00	7 00	7 00	7 00	1,000	10 00	10 25	10 75	
Canadian Western Bank	5,000	7 50	7 75	7 75	7 75	1,000	10 00	10 25	10 25	
Laurentian Bank	3,000	7 00	7 00	7 00	7 00	1,000	9 75	10 25	10 75	
Lloyds Bank Canada	5,000	7 25	7 50	7 50	7 50	1,000	10 00	10 25	10 75	
National Bank	5,000	7 00	7 00	7 00	7 00	1,000	9 75	10 25	10 75	
Royal Bank	5,000	7 00	7 00	7 00	7 00	1,000	10 00	10 25	10 75	
Toronto-Dominion Bank	5,000	7 00	7 00	7 00	7 00	1,000	10 00	10 25	10 75	
TRUST COMPANIES										
Canada Trust	5,000	8 00	8 00	8 00	8 25	1,000	10 00	10 25	10 75	
Central Trust	5,000	8 00	8 00	8 25	8 50	500	10 00	10 25	10 75	
Coronet Trust	10,000	9 25	9 50	9 75	9 75	2,000	10 50	10 75	10 87	
First City Trust	5,000	8 00	8 25	8 25	8 50	500	10 00	10 50	10 75	
General Trust	5,000	7 75	8 00	8 00	8 25	1,000	10 00	10 37	10 75	
Guaranty Trust	5,000	8 00	8 00	8 25	8 50	1,000	10 00	10 25	10 75	
Guardian Trust	5,000	8 75	8 75	9 00	9 00	1,000	10 00	10 37	10 87	
Household Trust	5,000	9 50	9 50	9 75	9 75	500	10 25	10 50	10 75	

week to Thursday September 29

Close	Change on week	Sales 100s		12 mo. HI Lo		Dividend	% Yield	Latest fiscal year earnings	Latest interim earnings	P/E ratio

A -B

Close	Change on week	Sales 100s		HI	Lo	Dividend	% Yield	Latest fiscal year earnings	Latest interim earnings	P/E ratio
1.75	-.05	64	AHA Auto Tch	6	1.60	.00	0	Dec87 .28	Jun6m .13	
0.18		30	Abbey Expl	55	18	.00	0			
1.00	-.10	57	Aber Res	2.30	1.00	.00	0		Apr3m .01D	
0.30		388	Abermin Corp	2.00	.27	.00	0	Dec87 .03D	Mar3m .01D	
20	-¼	463	Abitibi-Prce	35¾	19⅛	1.00	5.0	Dec87 1.70	Jun6m 1.37	8.7
1.03	-.17	197	Abitibi Wts	12	1.00	.00	0			
1.00	-.12	308	Acadia Mnl	4.55	1.00	.00	0			
0.62	-.03	7	Accgrph Cl A	3.60	.45	.00	0	Aug87 .60D	May9m .47D	
15⅛	⅜	599	Acklands	17⅛	14¼	.60	4.0	Nov87 .64	May6m .20	30.3

certainly want to follow his or her stocks in a daily newspaper. Otherwise, a weekly would suffice, as illustrated from the Financial Times, above.

Stock tables include trading information for the most recent period – including the share prices, price changes over the day (or week), the number of shares traded and the trading range during the past 12 months. They also include dividend information. The "indicated dividend," is the total dividend payment that would be paid over the next 12 months, based on the latest dividend declared by the company. The dividend may be paid quarterly, semi-annually or annually, depending on company policy.

The Toronto and Montreal stock exchange tables included in Financial Times give earnings information as well as financial ratios useful to investors. Two common ratios are yield and the price-earnings ratio. The yield is the dividend as a percentage of the stock price; the P/E ratio is the stock price divided by the latest 12-month earnings. So a P/E ratio of 12.7 means that an investor is paying $12.70 for each $1 of earnings.

TSE WEEKLY INDEX

	Week's close	Percent change from				P E ratio	Divi- dend yield%
		Last week	4 wks ago	52 wks ago	1988 High	Low		

	Week's close	Last week	4 wks ago	52 wks ago	1988 High	Low	P E ratio	Divi- dend yield%
Toronto 35	172.4	-0.6	-0.3	-16.5	-7.0	10.8	10.06	3.46
TSE 300	3261	-0.9	-0.4	-16.4	-6.3	9.6	10.91	3.35

Subindexes are ranked by change from 52 weeks ago, based on Thursday closings

	Week's close	Last week	4 wks ago	52 wks ago	1988 High	Low	P E ratio	Divi- dend yield%
Real Estate & Construction	14453	-0.5	-1.1	7.9	-3.0	27.1	38.97	1.38
Pipelines	3177	-0.5	-0.5	4.1	-6.5	26.3	15.78	4.85
Banks	2411	0.2	6.9	0.8	-1.4	27.4	7.35	5.06
Communications & Media	6937	1.0	4.7	-1.9	-0.9	19.2	19.25	1.90
Utilities	2626	-1.7	0.5	-3.3	-6.0	1.9	9.79	6.41
Financial Services	2365	0.1	5.1	-4.3	-1.2	23.4	7.90	4.82
Merchandising	3565	0.7	0.1	-5.1	-2.1	18.6	22.73	1.79
Integrated Oils	4056	-2.0	-3.9	-8.9	-5.4	19.2	13.14	3.07
Metals & Minerals	2747	-1.6	-2.3	-15.4	-14.9	22.8	7.40	2.84

Even if you don't follow individual stocks, you should keep an eye on the major stock market indexes. Virtually every major paper with a business section has a market summary graph and table (shown above) as well as a commentary on the latest developments.

Mutual fund investors can find a daily table of fund prices in most major papers. But most fund professionals use the Financial Times monthly survey of investment funds. It groups funds according to investment objectives, so you can compare your funds' performance against funds with similar objectives.

If you are an active investor in the U.S. markets, you'll probably want a paper with extensive U.S. stock trading information. This information is available in the Globe's Report on Business, the Wall Street Journal and Barron's, a U.S. financial weekly.

You'll also want a daily newspaper with complete tables if your investment interests extend to the options and futures markets. Because prices can be extremely volatile, you must remain well informed in order to make decisions quickly.

Corporate financial statements

Once you're adept at following business news and reading market tables, you should turn your attention to corporate financial statements. To do so, you don't have to become an expert investment analyst (and if all you ever plan to buy is Canada Savings Bonds, you can skip this section). But if you're interested in getting better returns on your investments than you've earned up to now, it's essential that you learn the basics of financial statements.

Table V

ABC Limited
Operating Statements for the Year Ended Dec. 31, 1987

	1987 ($000)	1986 ($000)
REVENUE		
Sales of products, fees earned	$150,000	$125,000
EXPENSES		
Cost of sales and services	$125,000	$110,000
Depreciation	4,000	3,500
Interest on long term debt	5,000	4,500
Other interest	2,000	1,500
TOTAL EXPENSES	136,000	119,500
Earnings before taxes	14,000	5,500
Taxes	6,000	3,000
NET EARNINGS	8,000	2,500
Earnings per share	$0.80	$0.25

Even if you plan to keep your money in any but the largest financial institutions or invest in corporate bonds, you should learn to read a company's financial report. It is rare for an institution to get into trouble overnight, so financial statements can offer valuable warnings of impending difficulties.

By law, every public company must issue an annual report covering financial results for its latest fiscal year. (The company must also provide updates through quarterly reports, although these contain less detail.) Companies selling securities to the public must issue a prospectus that includes the information a person needs to decide whether to invest.

Surprisingly, few people take the time to look at annual reports – which is a shame, because the information contained can help investors understand the company. Even if you don't examine the financial statements, the "management's discussion and financial review" section of the report is helpful because of its description of the company's operations and its essential information about earnings and developments. It, in effect, interprets the financial statements for the reader.

An annual report can generally be divided into a number of areas. The first is the report of the board of directors (or chairman's or president's report.) It usually reviews the company's operations during the year and often gives management's views of the outlook for the company and its industry. Of course, such reports try to show the company in a positive light.

Some investors ignore annual reports and financial statements because they expect their brokerage firm to deal with this information. In fact, the analysts employed by a brokerage house do watch for developments in companies whose shares have been recommended by the firm. Similarly, many people invest in mutual funds to have professional managers carry out all investment analysis for them. Even so, it makes sense to understand the basics so you can interpret results yourself; the experts aren't always right.

If you plan to invest in smaller companies you must learn to conduct your own analysis. While major brokerage houses follow major companies and provide detailed research reports, few provide studies of smaller firms. Sometimes the necessary information is not readily available, in which case the best advice is to stay away from the company – large or small – as an investment.

Financial statements may seem intimidating. But you'll see from the example in Table V on page 15 that they are valuable. The company, ABC Ltd., is fictitious and the statements are simplified. But by examining them you can see the basics that can be applied to analyzing genuine statements.

The first line includes the revenue the company received from the sale of its goods or services. From this, you subtract the company's expenses. The cost of goods and services includes the cost of goods sold, labor expenses, heat and light, rents, and so on.

Depreciation is a non-cash expense that takes into consideration wear and tear on equipment. For example, if a piece of machinery cost $1 million and has a lifespan of five years, it would be depreciated by $200,000 each year. That amount would be considered an expense, even though $200,000 wasn't spent. In our example the total depreciation charged in 1987 is $4 million.

The company may have financed its operations through a bond issue. The interest paid on this debt is shown separately from interest on short-term debt (usually bank borrowings). Bank borrowings can be repaid at any time; consequently they are considered short-term debt and would appear as "other interest."

Subtracting expenses from revenues results in pre-tax earnings. From these a company will pay taxes, leaving it with net earnings. Often a company will report current and deferred income taxes. Current taxes generally refer to those that are required for immediate tax purposes and deferred income taxes are generally segregated for accounting purposes.

Table VI

Balance Sheet as of Dec. 31, 1987
($000s)

	1987	1986
ASSETS		
Cash and investments	20,000	16,500
Inventory	30,000	10,000
Total current assets	50,000	26,500
Land	8,000	8,000
Buildings	40,500	42,500
Equipment	30,000	36,000
Less accumulated depreciation	12,000	8,000
Net fixed assets	66,500	78,500
Total assets	116,500	105,000
LIABILITIES		
Current liabilities	20,000	16,000
Bank loans	20,000	16,000
Total current liabilities	50,000	50,000
Long-term debt	70,000	66,000
SHAREHOLDERS' EQUITY		
Share Capital	20,000	20,000
Retained earnings	26,000	19,000
Total shareholders' equity	46,000	39,000
Total liabilities and shareholders' equity	116,000	105,000

Earnings per share represents total earnings divided by the number of shares outstanding. In this case we've assumed that the company has 10 million shares outstanding.

There are a number of profitability ratios investors can apply to the income statement. For example, you might look for trends of increased or decreased profitability by comparing the yearly change in the cost of goods sold as a percentage of revenues. Or you could compare this ratio with that of competing companies. Most important is the net profit margin – the percentage of earnings over revenues. Again compare this ratio against previous years and against similar companies, in order to find trends. This ratio varies from industry to industry and from company to company.

Retained earnings are the profits reinvested in the company. An example of a statement of retained earnings is shown in Table VII on the next page. This statement shows that of the $9 million profit, $2 million was paid out as dividends, leaving $7 million for reinvestment.

Table VII		
Statement of Retained Earnings ($000s)		
	1987	**1986**
Balance at beginning of year	$19,000	$17,000
Add net earnings	9,000	2,500
Less dividends paid	2,000	500
Balance at end of year	$26,000	$19,000

The balance sheet on page 17, a snapshot of the company's financial position Dec. 31, 1987, is broken into three sections: assets, liabilities and shareholders' equity.

The company's assets are divided into liquid assets – cash and assets that can be quickly turned to cash – and fixed assets such as buildings and machinery.

Liabilities are what the company owes. Current liabilities, such as bank loans, are liabilities that are due within one year. Long-term liabilities such as bonds and mortgages refer to debts that are due at some date beyond one year.

Shareholders' equity – the difference between assets and liabilities – is made up of share capital (the value of shares sold to the public, based on the price paid to the company rather than on market value) and retained earnings. Shareholders' equity generally grows by the amount of retained earnings.

There are a number of financial ratios that should be examined. One of the most important is the current ratio, which is current assets divided by current liabilities. In our case the current ratio is 1.5 to 1 – calculated by dividing $30 million by $20 million. The ratio indicates that the company has more than enough short-term assets available to pay off its current liabilities. Depending on the industry, a ratio of about to 1 to 1 is reason for concern, although in some cyclical industries investors would require a much higher ratio.

Another important yardstick is the debt-to-equity ratio. In our example, the value of outstanding long-term debt exceeds the value of fixed assets, with the ratio being about 1.13 to 1. This is acceptable in some industries, such as utilities, whose earnings are assured. It is not a healthy ratio for a company in a cyclical industry.

Analysis of financial ratios is extremely important for people investing in debt such as corporate bonds or in guaranteed investment certificates in excess of what is covered by deposit insurance. If you are going to invest in corporate bonds, your broker will be able to provide you with the information you need to judge the quality of the issue. But if you are in doubt or cannot understand what you are being told, stick with investments that are backed by government guarantees.

Another area of the annual report includes the financial statements. These consist of the balance sheet; the statement of earnings, which shows revenues, expenses and earnings or losses; the consolidated statement of retained earnings, which shows the portion of earnings retained or reinvested in the business; and the statement of changes in financial position, which shows how the company financed its operations.

The statements also include the auditors' report to the shareholders, which states that the company's independent auditors examined the statements in the annual report and are satisfied that they are accurate. Rarely will auditors make a qualified statement indicating concern about a company's viability as an ongoing concern. When they do, it is a warning that should not be ignored. It is not the auditors' job to look for fraud; instead, they review how the company prepared its statements and decide whether they are reasonable.

The statements also include a series of notes which give substantial information about the company's accounting policies, transactions involving officers and directors, important lawsuits (if any) and information on long-term commitments such as leases. Reading these helps build your understanding of the company.

After you've learned enough about statement analysis to enable you to ask securities salespeople the right questions, you are ready for the next step: learning the basics of the types of investments offered in Canada.

Debt vs. equity

There are two major categories of investment. One is debt, the other is equity.

In the case of debt, you lend your money to a government, corporation or individual. In return you are promised the payment of interest and the return of your principal at the end of a set period. Common examples are savings accounts, Canada Savings Bonds and GICs.

How safe your money is depends on the financial strength of the issuer and whether your funds are insured or guaranteed by a third party. Money on deposit in Canada with a bank or trust company is insured for up to $60,000 in principal and interest per institution by the Canada Deposit Insurance Corp. (more on it later). Credit unions have a similar arrangement. Canada Savings Bonds are guaranteed by the federal government, so they are practically risk free. Some bonds are secured by specific assets, just like a mortgage is secured by property.

Some debt instruments, however, are a lot safer than others. For example, the subsidiaries of Principal Group that offered investment certificates may have guaranteed these instruments, but their guarantees were worthless when the Edmonton-based parent company ran into serious financial difficulties.

Here's a good rule to follow: If you aren't going to take the time to analyze the creditworthiness of an issuer of debt, stick with deposits that are backed by a government guarantee or are insured. For amounts above those covered by deposit insurance, stick with the largest banks and trust companies.

As noted earlier, lenders invest in debt. But if you invest in equity, such as common stocks, you become an owner and participate in the profits of enterprises. If you choose your investments carefully, you will profit through gains in their value and increased cash flow through dividend payments.

Historically, people who have invested for growth have earned returns of several percentage points a year more than those who have invested for income. That, of course, is a broad generalization. Many people have become wealthy through prudent investment and earned returns far in excess of what would have been earned investing in a broadly based portfolio.

Conversely, many people lost because they failed to analyze, because they listened to bad investment tips, or because they failed to monitor their holdings. It's possible to lose on so-called "safe investments" as well. And that brings us to the next part of this book – how the government taxes your investment income.

CHAPTER THREE

TAX RULES: INCREASING YOUR TAKE

IT IS ESSENTIAL THAT AS AN INVESTOR, YOU DEVELOP A BASIC UNDERstanding of the income tax system and how it applies to investment income. Otherwise you could end up paying more tax than you should.

There are two key points to consider: how different types of investment income are taxed, and what you can and cannot do to split income among family members for tax purposes.

Beginning in 1988, Canadians have three tax brackets, down from the previous 10. New federal income tax rates are 17% on the first $27,500 of taxable income, 26% on taxable income from $27,501 to $55,000 and 29% on anything more than $55,000. Your federal tax will also be reduced by tax credits. For example, all taxpayers receive a basic personal tax credit, which replaces the former basic personal deduction. Depending on your circumstances, you may be eligible for other credits, such as those for child support or spousal support.

In addition to federal tax, you must pay provincial tax of about half the federal rate (it varies from province to province). So if your top marginal federal tax rate is 26%, your combined top federal-provincial rate will be about 39% (not including surtaxes); if your top federal rate is 29%, your combined federal-provincial rate will be about 43.5%.

The taxes you pay on money earned through investment depend not only on your marginal tax rate, but on the source of the investment income. Interest and dividends from foreign corporations are the most heavily taxed, followed by Canadian dividends and capital gains.

You'll pay your full marginal tax rate on interest income and on dividends from foreign companies (either paid directly to you or through a mutual fund). So if you have $1,000 of interest income and your marginal tax rate is 39%, the tax bill comes to $390. Until 1988, the first

Table VIII

A Comparison of the Taxation of $100 of Interest
Income with $100 of Dividend Income

	Interest	Dividend
Interest received	$100.00	
Dividend received		$100.00
Dividend "gross-up"		25.00
Taxable dividend		125.00
Federal tax (29%)	29.00	36.35
Less: Dividend tax credit		16.67
Net federal tax	29.00	19.58
Add: Provincial tax	14.50	9.79
Total tax	44.37	29.37
Net: After Tax	$55.63	$70.63

$1,000 of interest income was effectively exempt from tax because of an investment income deduction that disappeared with tax reform.

Dividends from Canadian corporations are treated differently. This treatment is designed to reflect the fact that dividends are paid from profits that in most cases have already been taxed, and to encourage investors to invest in common and preferred shares. If you receive dividends from Canadian corporations, your tax rate on those payments will be reduced by the federal dividend tax credit.

Calculating the tax on dividends can be complicated. The amount on which you base your federal tax calculation is 125% of the actual dividend received – known as the "grossed-up" figure. So if you receive $100 in dividends, this figure is increased by 25% to $125, against which you calculate federal tax. From this figure you subtract the dividend tax credit, which is 13.33% of the grossed-up dividend (or 16.67% of the dividend actually received). This amount is then subtracted from your federal tax.

Table VIII compares the taxation of interest and dividend income. The calculation assumes the investor pays tax at the top marginal rate and has a provincial tax rate of 50% of the federal rate. For the purposes of this example, surtaxes are ignored.

In the end, the dividend tax credit reduces the tax you pay on dividends from Canadian corporations so that on a before-tax basis $1 of dividends is equal to about $1.26 of interest – a ratio that holds true no matter which federal tax bracket you're in. As a result, a 6.4% after-tax dividend is equal to an 8% interest-rate yield, while an 8% dividend is equal to a 10% interest-rate yield and a 12% dividend is equal to a 15% interest yield.

(If you live in Quebec, you'll find some variance in your after-tax interest and dividend income because the province sets its own income tax rates, independent of federal rates. A Quebec resident paying the top federal and provincial tax rates would net about $49 from $100 of interest income and about $61 from $100 of dividend income.)

Capital gains are taxed differently. First, it is comforting to know that the first third of capital gains earned is untaxed, leaving only 66.67% unsheltered from the taxman's grasp. Therefore, if you have $100 of capital gains, $66.67 is taxable. If you're paying the top marginal tax rate, that will result in tax of $29.58 and net earnings of $70.32. However, this formula applies only for 1988 and 1989. Beginning in 1990, the first 25% of capital gains will be exempt from tax. At that point, with $100 of capital gains you'll pay tax on $75, which at the top marginal tax rate would cost you $33.28, leaving $66.72.

Ottawa allows each taxpayer a lifetime capital gains exemption of $100,000. This applies to gross capital gains, as opposed to taxable capital gains, and affects just about any capital gain you earn – including stock market profits, gains from the sale of a family cottage and profits from selling precious metals. Gains from the sale of a family's principal residence are exempt from tax and have no bearing on the lifetime exemption.

Many people try to structure their finances to take advantage of the lifetime exemption by purchasing investments such as stocks and mutual funds that have the potential to generate capital gains. Some people use borrowed funds because the interest paid on amounts borrowed for investment is deductible from income for tax purposes. However, if borrowed funds are used and interest expenses exceed dividend and interest income, you will be required to pay tax on a portion of taxable capital gains equal to your "cumulative net investment loss" (which also includes certain writeoffs stemming from tax shelter investments). Tax must be paid on this portion of capital gains even if you have yet to use all of your lifetime capital gains exemption. But you won't lose your exemption; you'll just postpone your ability to use it until you have taxable capital gains that exceed your "cumulative net investment losses."

Let's assume that you have not used any of your lifetime exemption and you have $100,000 of gross realized capital gains for 1988, plus interest expense of $12,000. Because only 66.67% of capital gains is taxable, you will pay no tax on $33,333 of that gain. That leaves $66,667 as taxable income. But because you have not used any of your $100,000 lifetime

Table IX

Using Leverage to Invest

	Without Leverage	With Leverage
Investment	$100,000	$100,000
Loan	–	100,000
Cash flow at yearend	7,320	–
Interest (Pre-tax)	–	12,000
Capital gain (15%)	15,000	30,000
WITH LIFETIME EXEMPTION		
Equity after one year	122,320	130,000
Capital gain	15,000	30,000
Taxable gain (66.7%)	10,000	20,000
Taxable portion		
(equal to interest expense)		12,000
Tax (39% of $12,000)	–	4,680
After-tax profit	15,000	25,320
Add: cash flow	7,320	–
INCREASE IN NET WORTH	22,320	25,320
WITHOUT LIFETIME EXEMPTION		
Equity after one-year	122,320	130,000
Capital gain	15,000	30,000
Taxable gain (66.7%)	10,000	20,000
Tax (39%)	3,900	7,800
After-tax profit	11,100	22,200
Add: cash flow	7,320	–
INCREASE IN NET WORTH	$18,420	$22,200

capital gains exemption you can use it to reduce taxes. Of your $66,667 taxable capital gain, all but $12,000 – an amount equal to your cumulative investment loss – will be free of tax. And you'll be able to use the remaining portion of your lifetime exemption in subsequent years.

If you have not used all your lifetime exemption and you have cumulative investment losses, you need to make some tough decisions. In many cases, investors are better off not borrowing for investment until they have exhausted their lifetime exemption. Still, it depends largely on the expected rate of return that will be earned on the borrowed funds, so there are no hard rules. Investors in this situation should assess how they would fare with borrowed funds and compare the results with those likely through the use of their own capital.

Table IX above, compares the results of two investments over one year. In the first case, an investor uses $100,000 of his own money; in the second case he uses $100,000 of his own money, plus $100,000 of borrowed funds. In the second instance $12,000 of tax-deductible interest is paid to the lender. Because this amount is tax deductible, it has an after-tax value of $7,320, which we will assume is available for investment in the first example.

In addition to understanding how investment income is taxed, you should be aware of how Ottawa treats income within a family.

In most cases, income is taxed in the hands of the person who earns it, and income from investments is taxed in the hands of the person who provides the capital. In other words, you cannot give your spouse capital for investment and expect to have the income taxed at his or her marginal tax rate. That's because Ottawa will consider the income yours and hold you responsible for paying tax on it.

That's the simplest case. Things become more complicated if, for instance, you provide your spouse with financial backing to open a business he or she will operate. In such a case, you should seek professional accounting and legal advice.

If you give or lend funds to your children, grandchildren, nieces or nephews under the age of 18, the rules are again somewhat different. Interest and dividends are taxable in your hands, but capital gains are taxable in the hands of the children. Even more complicated is the fact that interest earned on interest (on which you have paid tax) is taxable in the children's hands.

If you invest family allowance cheques on behalf of a child by depositing the payments directly to an account in the child's name, the interest earned is taxable in the child's hands. Because a child can earn several thousand dollars without affecting your ability to claim that child as a deduction, this income can effectively be tax free.

These income-attribution rules affect spouses and children under 18. If you give or lend funds to common-law spouses and adult children, income will be taxed in their hands, not yours.

The attribution rules make it necessary for families to engage in long-term investment planning if they are to make wise use of their money. Ideally, each spouse should have approximately the same amount of investment assets. So if a woman plans to leave the workforce to have children it might make sense for her to save her entire salary and for the couple to use the husband's income to pay expenses. Then, at a later date, he would build up his investment capital. This way, income earned by the wife will likely be taxed at a lower rate than if all the family investment income were taxed in the husband's hands.

Income-splitting was at one time a popular tax-saving strategy, but Ottawa has eliminated most opportunities to split income. However, there are still some ways of selling assets to a family member at fair market value to generate capital that can be invested. Again, if you are thinking about taking this route, you should seek professional advice.

CHAPTER FOUR

FIRST THINGS FIRST

BEFORE STARTING YOUR INVESTMENT PROGRAM, THERE ARE SOME ESsential steps you should follow to ensure your financial well-being. One of the first is to dispose of all non-productive personal debts – in other words, all debts not used to purchase investment assets such as securities or real assets such as a home or cottage. Personal debts are the biggest barrier to building substantial assets.

Consumer credit is very expensive. The cost of carrying an unpaid balance on a credit card can be as much as 2% a month. On an average balance of $1,000 a month, that adds up to about $240 a year in interest. Moreover, the interest on personal debt is not deductible from income, which means you must earn a great deal more than $240 to pay that interest. For example, if your marginal tax rate is 39%, almost $400 of your gross income goes to paying the interest on that $1,000. It is easy to see, then, why the best investment you can make is to pay down that debt. You will not find a stock market investment that can give you a consistent rate of return that exceeds the cost of consumer debt.

Still, it is unrealistic to expect most people to stay out of debt completely. Credit is necessary in many cases, particularly for big-ticket items such as cars and houses. The trick is to keep debt costs to a minimum, and that means paying off your most expensive forms of credit first. You should, therefore, try to pay off your credit card debt as soon as possible, and then make a habit of paying off balances in full each month. Credit cards should never be used as a source of financing, but instead as a convenient alternative to carrying cash or a cheque book. If it is impossible to pay off the balance, it is better to borrow the necessary funds elsewhere at less cost. You are much better off using a bank personal line of credit, which offers substantially lower interest rates – generally a percentage point or two above the prime lending rate. This could cut interest expenses by as much as one-half.

And if you are in the market for a loan, shop around. The cost of credit varies widely, so if your own bank, trust company or financial institution is not the least expensive, ask it to match the best rate you can find. If it will not, consider going elsewhere. Similarly, mortgage rates can differ among institutions. Even a small fraction of a percentage point can make a significant difference in payments, especially on a large mortgage. Again, your best bet is to shop for the lowest rate possible, particularly if you are buying a new home. Changing mortgage companies to get a lower rate when it's time to renew a mortgage can be expensive because of legal costs, so shopping at that time may not be so advantageous. In this case the best route may be to ask your current mortgage-holder to match the lowest available rate.

Invest now, or pay off your debts?

Of course, you should strive to pay down your debts as quickly as possible. The quicker you do, the more money you'll have in your pocket for savings, investment or spending. However, many people feel they can do better by using their savings to play the stock market, rather than by eliminating debts.

Perhaps they can. But market performance figures suggest that the average investor certainly cannot. Even so, you may be confident you're a member of the minority that can realize a better return on stocks than you would get by paying down debt. Yet even in this case, it makes sense to structure your finances to cut your interest expenses.

First, use your savings or cash flow to pay off debts. Then borrow the funds back to buy stocks or other investments. You'll still owe the same amount but you'll reap additional gains at tax time. Because your loan is now for investments, the interest is deductible from income for tax purposes. But you must be prepared to show that the loan is, in fact, for investment – meaning you must have documentation to prove the money was borrowed to buy an investment and that it was used for an investment. And remember: if you want to deduct interest, your investment must be made with the expectation of producing income in the form of interest or dividends. So while stocks qualify – even if it is unlikely that they will pay dividends – gold bullion does not. That's because gold will never pay a dividend.

If you plan to restructure your affairs to make your interest deductible, you're probably best off reviewing the procedure with your financial advisor to ensure you have the proper documentation and that you will not run afoul of Ottawa's anti-avoidance tax rules.

Deciding whether you should borrow for investment is another matter. Certainly, fortunes have been made by those who operate with borrowed funds – and fortunes have been lost as well. For example, most real estate purchases are heavily leveraged, meaning investors provide some of their own capital, but borrow a great deal more. In the case of commercial real estate, deals are often financed 80% or more with borrowed capital. Stock market purchases can also be leveraged, but stock exchange bylaws limit the portion of borrowed funds to 50% (or less in the case of more risky junior securities). Many sellers of mutual funds also recommend purchasing funds with borrowed money, and a number of financial institutions have arrangements with mutual fund dealers to provide financing for purchases of up to $3 for every $1 the client invests.

But markets move down as well as up, and if you are heavily leveraged a price drop could cause significant problems. If you buy securities with borrowed funds and the price of your investment declines you must come up with more capital so that the equity in your account meets the minimum under your purchase agreement. In the case of stocks, equity must at least equal the amount owed to your broker. In the case of real estate, the investor must come up with funds to pay interest on debt if the cash flow fails to cover costs.

So while leverage can make you a lot of money, it can also be a losing strategy. If you decide to use borrowed funds for investment, make sure you understand the risks and have the financial strength to keep yourself above water if your investment goes sour. It's best not to get in over your head when you borrow – that is, if you must borrow at all.

Choosing an investment advisor

Choosing a stockbroker, mutual fund dealer or any other investment professional is one of the most important investment decisions you will make. Even the most sophisticated investors need brokers or other intermediaries, if only to execute orders properly and pass on information. Novice investors, meanwhile, must depend heavily on brokers and other investment salespeople for advice, suggestions and guidance about specific securities and an overall investment strategy.

The choice of advisors has become more complicated in recent years with the introduction of specialized financial products such as options and futures on treasury bills, bonds, currencies and stock market indexes. Even "basic" financial products such as stocks, bonds, and mutual funds have become increasingly complex. As a result, an investor who diversifies

– for example, with a portfolio including stocks, mutual funds, futures, options and bonds – can find himself dealing with several investment professionals.

Further complicating matters is the fact that since 1983 brokerage firms have been allowed to set their own commission rates, rather than adhering to a fixed-rate schedule set by major stock exchanges. A number of discount brokerage firms have opened shop, charging commissions of as little as one-fifth of the old fixed schedule for large orders. But unlike traditional brokerage firms, they offer few services other than the execution of orders. (The discounters are looking at adding some services in the hopes of attracting additional business and improving profitability.) They appeal mostly to investors who conduct their own research and analysis and who don't want pay for brokerage house research.

However, the majority of investors choose to deal with brokerage firms that can provide a variety of services and products, or with those that specialize in specific products. These firms should continually provide clients with essential information that affects their holdings, as well as keeping them informed of new investment opportunities. In other words, the brokerage houses should be more than simple order takers.

Not all full-service firms are alike. Some are major underwriting firms, which raise capital for corporations by selling new securities to financial institutions and the public. These firms are often owned or controlled by major financial institutions, and they also have large retail operations to handle trading for individuals. Within these retail operations are often found departments that specialize in mutual funds, commodities and options trading.

Other firms specialize in providing trading expertise and independent research to clients and do not get heavily involved in underwriting. Most of these firms deal almost exclusively with institutional investors such as pension funds, insurance companies, banks, mutual funds and trust companies. However, some actively pursue retail business and may even take part in some underwritings through a "selling group." While they are not involved in putting the underwriting together or in financing a major part of it, they are involved in the distribution of securities.

Mutual fund dealers are a somewhat different breed. Most call themselves financial planners and try to work out long-term investment programs aimed at meeting clients' financial goals. Financial planners often are licensed to sell insurance as well as mutual funds, while some also offer tax-shelter products. In addition, major insurance companies have also been entering the mutual fund market in recent years.

There are two types of mutual fund dealers. The first includes those that are part of a direct selling force and sell only products belonging to one group of funds. Generally, commissions charged by these dealers are fixed.

The second type of is the independent dealer that sells funds offered by several fund management companies. In theory, such dealers can choose from among several hundred funds, but in practice they usually limit their selection to a handful. Commissions are negotiable, although many independent dealers, and particularly those that offer detailed financial planning services, are unwilling to trim fees substantially.

Choosing a brokerage firm

Before choosing a brokerage firm you should decide on your main investment objective. For example, people whose interests include substantial dealings in bonds are probably wise to consider large, integrated firms. Because of their underwriting business, they have major bond trading departments and are better equipped to buy and sell bonds than most small investment dealers.

If stocks are your priority, it's wise to make sure the firm you deal with is a member of the Toronto Stock Exchange (or in Quebec, the Montreal Exchange). Such memberships indicate the firm has direct access to the most important Canadian securities markets.

TSE members dealing with retail investors range in size from small firms with a handful of personnel in one office to large firms with offices in major centres across the country. Large firms usually provide a wide variety of research products, ranging from economic analysis to detailed reports on individual industry groups and stocks. However, they cannot be expected to follow many of the smaller publicly traded companies because it would not be a cost-effective use of their analysts' time. Instead, they follow more established companies that are more likely to be of interest to clients.

They may follow smaller companies as part of an industry group or as a "special situation." But their emphasis is almost always on larger, more heavily traded stocks.

Possible conflicts of interest

The salespeople at large firms are often not allowed to recommend stocks not followed closely by their analysts. As a result, their clients probably will not hear of many investment oportunities. In addition, because these dealers tend to track the same companies, information they distribute is rarely unique and is usually reflected in the price of a stock before clients have access to the research reports.

A second area of concern for investors is the possible conflict between the underwriting and sales departments of major firms. Dealers deny there is a problem, yet it is rare that a brokerage house will issue a negative report on a company that is an important underwriting client of the firm.

Investors should also realize that not all clients get information at the same time. A firm will be in contact more often with a client who generates $25,000 in yearly commissions than one whose small portfolio results in $100 in revenues.

Large clients, especially portfolio managers with financial institutions, are constantly in touch with brokerage house analysts and often benefit from analysts' views long before they are in print. Most firms have designed ways to pass on analysts' opinions to retail sales representatives quickly, but small clients still get the last phone call – if they are called at all.

For that reason, small investors with only a few thousand dollars to invest in stocks and who are not likely to have large portfolios down the road are probably better off in a mutual fund. On the other hand, if you're capable of doing your own analysis and are assertive enough to pester your broker for information, you might consider individual investments. Even then you should look at the economics of being a small investor in the stock market. If you have only $1,000 and want to split it between two stocks, you'll have to pay two minimum commission fees, which are likely be about $50 each. And you'll have to pay a commission when you sell, too.

Small brokerage houses usually follow the same pecking order when it comes to calling clients. The call made first is the one that is most likely to result in an order. But smaller houses usually have fewer underwriting ties, and as a result are more inclined to give impartial advice. Smaller dealers may also compensate for offering fewer services by following companies ignored by their larger competitors, bringing their clients superior opportunities for gains. Most firms offer research on individual stocks, but major integrated brokerage houses usually produce much more written information covering the economy, the bond market and preferred shares.

The sales representative

There are thousands of people across Canada who are licensed to sell securities to the public. Some perform their duties superbly, while some are inept. But, as is the case with most professions, most are adequate for the job.

You should, therefore, give at least as much thought to selecting a broker or other investment advisor as you would to choosing a doctor. If you know your investment objectives, your first step is to screen a number of dealers to find some that offer the services you require. A phone call to retail sales managers at most firms will get you much of the information you need for a preliminary screening. But face-to-face visits are best. You should be prepared to discuss your investment objectives and financial needs openly. If a firm appears able to provide the services you're looking for, its sales manager will usually try to introduce you to a sales representative with whom you seem compatible. If you have only a few thousand dollars you will likely be matched to the "broker of the day" – the person selected to meet most walk-in clients on a particular day.

You should determine how much experience a sales representative has. There is no substitute for experience, so it is usually desirable to deal with someone who has several years of exposure to the markets, and who has worked in times of both rising and falling prices. Many less-experienced brokers were shell-shocked when the market fell in October 1987; after five years of rising prices it was their first experience with a rapid decline.

You should ask for copies of past research reports sent to clients and study them carefully to determine whether the recommendations have helped clients' portfolios outperform the market. Ask the representative whether he or she sticks with the company list or conducts independent research. Find out how the firm deals with sell recommendations of shares of companies that are underwriting clients. In addition, ask the representative for the names of several clients you can contact for an assessment of the firm's and the sales representative's track records. In your conversations with the representative determine his interests in the market. If he has expertise in junior speculative situations and you want a low-risk portfolio, find someone else. In addition, ask whether you can expect much in the way of personal service based on the size of your account. Some firms discourage their employees from taking on new small accounts because the commissions hardly cover the cost of executing the transaction. No experienced broker can afford the time to service a small account that has little chance of growing.

Placing an order

Clients who understand basic stock market terminology stand a better chance of avoiding confusion when placing orders to buy or sell securities. It is, after all, of utmost importance that your sales representative fully understand your instructions. There should be no confusion about the number of shares being bought or sold. Unless your order is "at the market" – the best price the broker can get at the time – the client should specify a buying or selling price. Furthermore, you must decide whether the order is a day order – one that must be resubmitted each day until the stock is bought or sold – or an open order that remains in effect until the transaction is complete. Many people deal with more than one sales representative, so it is essential that the order be placed with only one.

Sometimes disputes develop between a representative and a client over what was said. This breakdown of communications can usually be prevented by being explicit when placing an order. You should keep notes that contain the date and time the order was placed and the instructions given the broker – including whether the order was to buy or sell, the full name of the stock and the price. Make sure you receive progress reports on your orders during the day and at the close of trading. If a problem develops, talk to your representative first. If a solution cannot be reached, speak with the office's retail sales manager. If that doesn't work, try the stock exchange involved or, as a last resort, your provincial securities commission. But remember, even though orders are not in writing, they are legally binding contracts.

Types of accounts

Brokerage firms offer clients several types of accounts, including cash accounts, delivery - against - payment accounts (DAP) and margin accounts. With cash accounts, clients pay for their shares on settlement date, which is five business days after a transaction is made. They can either take possession of their share certificates or leave them with the brokerage firm for safekeeping. Discount brokers offer fewer options. Generally they require that clients have adequate cash in their accounts before placing an order to buy stock. Similarly, they require that shares be in the firm's possession before accepting an order to sell.

In the case of DAP accounts, a broker delivers the securities to the client's bank or trust company in exchange for payment. As a result, DAP accounts are mainly employed by institutional investors, but some individuals also use them. With margin accounts, part of the purchase price of the shares is made with funds borrowed from the brokerage firm. The purchased securities remain in the hands of the firm and can be used as collateral for loans used to finance the firm's operations. Fully paid securities are segregated from those that can be used as collateral.

Each type of account has its pros and cons. However, DAP accounts, although they are inconvenient for brokers and involve some extra expenses for clients, are the safest.

The question then becomes, how safe is safe? Clients – and potential customers – can take some solace in the fact that there have been few major financial disasters in the Canadian brokerage industry. The demise of Osler Inc. of Toronto in early 1988 caused some inconvenience and resulted in plenty of publicity, but individual clients didn't suffer any financial losses. The previous notable failure – Malone Lynch – in 1972 again resulted in no individual losses. However, individuals with margined positions had their holdings liquidated and they were paid the resulting cash value.

Protection limited

Should a firm fail, investors are protected by the National Contingency Fund, established by the brokerage industry to protect clients against losses. However, the fund appears to have its limits.

If you worry about margin accounts, the only alternative is to use a bank line of credit. Investors who trade frequently and on margin do not have an alternative to margin accounts unless they arrange their own bank financing and deliveries. Interest paid on money borrowed to buy shares is deductible for tax purposes, but it is important that detailed records be kept; otherwise, Ottawa may disallow the expense. If you choose a cash or DAP account and plan to keep your shares for some time, they should be fully registered in your name. This assures that you will get all company information and dividends directly, although investment dealers will collect these on your behalf and credit your account if the shares are in the brokerage firm's (or "street") name. Since early 1988, brokers have been required to send copies of company reports to clients whose holdings are in the broker's name.

Monitoring performance

Once an account has been established, it is important that the client monitor the broker's performance. As a client, you should ensure you are benefiting from the research you were promised and that you are getting personal service. You should also monitor the success of your broker's recommendations, and record whether you acted on them. Determine whether they brought higher returns than had you left your portfolio alone. And if you suspect your representative is making recommendations for your account for the sole purpose of generating commissions –

known as churning – then it's time to move on. The alternative is to learn to make your own investment decisions or move into a mutual fund.

The funds alternative

If you're a smaller investor, your broker might recommend that you invest in a mutual fund (also known as an investment fund). If you decide funds are for you, and you intend to buy from your brokerage firm instead of a mutual fund dealer, make sure the sales representative you choose is a specialist. Anyone can buy into a fund for clients, but it makes sense to use those who closely monitor the objectives and performance of fund management companies. An investment advisor should also help clients determine how funds can be used as part of a total savings and financial planning program and to find funds that meet clients' objectives. And the selection criteria for stockbrokers are just as applicable to those who sell mutual funds. Client names should be requested and references checked. It is important, too, that you determine what type of service you will receive. Will it be a once-a-year telephone call or a more involved relationship?

The cost in commissions

Commission rates on all but a few funds are negotiable, and virtually all have sliding commission schedules which vary according to the size of the order. So when it all adds up, the commission rate you pay may be a lot less than the 9% maximum. Discount brokers, on the other hand, will generally charge half of the maximum commission for a given order. But if you do not require advice or service, most fund dealers or brokerage firms will match the discounter.

Whether you can obtain a discount if you require detailed advice depends largely on the circumstances and the policies of the company you deal with. Some may discount commissions drastically if you redeem money in one fund and reinvest in another; yet on a new investment they may charge full commission. It's best to discuss fees in advance so you won't face any surprises.

Financial planners

Some investment professionals call themselves financial planners. Rather than simply selling a financial product, they analyze their clients' financial situations, review their objectives and develop a plan aimed at fulfilling these objectives. Areas to be considered include debt management, life insurance, retirement savings and general investment. Some financial planners operate on a fee-for-service basis and accept no commissions. However, most charge no fee but receive a commission if you buy a financial product through them. If you deal with a financial planner, make sure you understand the ground rules so you can determine whether he'll give objective advice.

First, you should note that anyone can call himself a financial planner. This is a serious problem because it allows people who have no training or experience to hang a shingle suggesting some expertise in the area of finance. As a result, it is best to determine what qualifications a financial planner has. The CFP (Chartered Financial Planner) designation after the planner's name means he has completed a series of industry courses leading to the designation. The Canadian Association of Financial Planners also sets minimum standards for membership.

Preparing a will

It is essential that you have a will. But even if you do, that does not mean you should set it aside and ignore it. Your will should be reviewed periodically to ensure it continues to reflect your wishes and conforms to the laws of the province in which you live. For example, Ontario's Family Law Reform Act changed the rules dramatically for many people. As well, federal legislation passed in September, 1988, allowed RRSP holders to name common-law spouses as beneficiaries. This will require many Canadians to review their wills. The objective of a will, and estate planning, is to make sure your assets are distributed according to your wishes after you die, while keeping the tax bite to a minimum.

While the $100,000 lifetime capital gains exemption simplifies estate planning for many people (because it covers family assets such as cottages that are allowed to pass tax free from one generation to another) a will is still necessary. Even modest estates require the clarification a professionally prepared will can provide.

When preparing your will, make sure your lawyer has copies of important investment documents, such as a copy of the beneficiary form you may have signed when you opened an RRSP.

Life insurance

Life and disability insurance are also key planks in any financial strategy. As such, they should be taken care of before setting up an investment program. It is best to first determine how much insurance is necessary to maintain your family's standard of living should anything happen to you. There are no hard-and-fast rules about adequate coverage, but many advisors suggest life insurance of 10 times annual income, plus enough funds to pay off debts.

In any event, life insurance is a product offered by dozens of major companies. And like any other financial product, quality and price vary widely – so it makes sense to shop around and to ask agents for comparisons of companies and products. Some agents handle insurance products issued by only one company, while others deal with several companies or provide computerized price comparisons of similar products. You should also consider the differences between term insurance (insurance that covers you for a specific period) and whole life insurance (insurance that covers you for life and which contains a so-called "savings" element).

CHAPTER FIVE

SETTING YOUR INVESTMENT OBJECTIVES

ONCE YOU'VE GOT YOUR HOUSE IN ORDER AND HAVE COVERED THE basics, you're ready for the next step – defining your investment objectives and meeting them. This means deciding how much money you'll need on a certain date for a certain purpose and structuring your financial affairs to meet that goal.

For example, you may decide that in two years you'll need $50,000 for a down payment on a home. Or you may have a longer-term goal in mind, such as saving enough for a comfortable retirement.

Meeting your goal of a down payment may not be easy; after all, you have to sock away the money. But it is more straightforward than making adequate provisions for retirement. What happens, for instance, if you decide you want to retire 20 years from now on $50,000 a year? Thanks to inflation, the major difficulty is determining how much you will need 20 years from now to provide the equivalent of $50,000 of today's purchasing power. You must also estimate the rates of return that you're likely to receive from your investments over the next two decades.

What's more, you may have a number of goals in mind, not all of which are complementary. You may want to make accelerated mortgage payments, contribute the maximum to your RRSP and set aside funds for children's education – only to find that doing all three would constitute an impossible drain on your finances. As a result, you must consider making some tradeoffs and establishing priorities.

The most common investment objectives are: saving for retirement, saving for children's education, saving to buy a home or cottage, saving to buy a business, and simply accumulating capital. Some people might even want to speculate with a portion of their assets in the hope of making gains quickly, although it is wise to ensure your more conservative investment programs are in place before you engage in speculative investing. Investment objectives can often be divided into short-term and long-term objectives. The major difference, obviously, is the period of time the investment will cover. On the short-term side, someone saving to accumulate the down payment on a house might want access to his or her money within a year or two. Conversely, someone saving for retirement might expect to wait 20 years or so before making use of the funds – a long-term proposition.

The level of risk

Timing leads to other important differences, the most crucial being the level of risk you should assume when setting your objectives. As was noted in Chapter 1, different types of investments provide different returns. Guaranteed investments are safest because you know the rate of return in advance. So if you put your money in a one-year term deposit, you are assured that at the end of the year you'll get all your capital back, plus the stated amount of interest. But if you sink your money into a mutual fund that invests in Canadian stocks, you have little idea what you will earn.

Historically, long-term investors in such funds, or in diversified portfolios of Canadian common stocks, have realized returns substantially higher than those for guaranteed investments. Many funds have 10-year average annual compound rates of return in excess of 15%. But year-to-year rates vary widely. In most years they've exceeded the rates available from guaranteed returns, although in some years they've been lower.

It makes sense, then, that the person expecting to need money in a year or so is better off with a guaranteed investment. The person with a longer-term horizon, perhaps five to 10 years or longer, is able to accept more risk and varied of rates of return. Therefore, he should consider investments with growth potential.

For long-term investors, higher rates of return make a significant difference in the amount of money accumulated over time. If $1,000 is set aside each year for 20 years at an annual average interest rate of 8%, it will grow to $49,423. But a rate of 14% would result in $103,768 after 20 years. Even for a single investment of $1,000, the difference can be substantial. That single deposit, earning 8%, would be worth $4,661 after 20 years. At a 14% growth rate it would be worth $13,743.

If a guaranteed rate of return appeals to you, you can lock away your money for a relatively long period. You might, for instance, buy government bonds for 20 years or longer. They pay significantly higher rates of return than treasury bills, but the rate remains static for the entire period. That's good news if interest rates fall, but if they rise investors may find themselves wishing they had taken another course of action.

When possible, investors should aim for growth. While growth investments are riskier because their returns are unpredictable, investors are usually compensated for this risk through greater gains. Conversely, investors with short-term goals should play it safe.

No matter what route you choose, investment options are available to help you meet your goals. For safety, many people choose run-of-the-mill bank accounts. But why not consider alternatives that are just as secure? They include bank premium savings accounts, trust company and credit union accounts, term deposits, treasury bills and money market funds. All are risk free, within limits, but rates paid vary significantly.

Saving to meet a specific objective can also involve a great deal more than investing for growth or income. You can make use of programs and tax breaks that can help increase returns without increasing risk. Saving for retirement and saving for children's education are two goals for which tax-assisted savings schemes are available.

Saving for retirement

Most people are eager to embark on a savings program that will allow them to live comfortably during retirement. This is recognized by the federal government through tax legislation that encourages companies to implement pension plans and allows individuals to save for retirement through registered retirement savings plans.

Because government pension benefits alone are inadequate for most people during retirement, private pension plans are an excellent method of ensuring that the income you need will be available. Trouble is, many companies don't have pension plans. And if they do, the plans may prove woefully inadequate. So taking retirement savings into your own hands may be the best solution to financial freedom during your golden years.

If this is the case, there are three cardinal rules to remember: Save as much as you can, start as early as you can, and aim for growth. Starting early is the key, simply because it puts the power of compound interest at your command. The 25-year-old who sets aside $1,000 a year at an 8% annual return will have $186,000 at age 60. The 45-year-old who wants the same amount at age 60 will have to set aside more than $6,000 a year. Furthermore, if the 25-year-old could earn 12% annually, he would accumulate $483,000 by age 60.

It's never too late to start. If you haven't saved for retirement until now, you can still reap the benefits of an improving government regulatory climate for retirement savings. For one thing, pension plans are changing. Legislation proposed by Ottawa improves the portability of pension plans and enhances survivor benefits.

Even so, this means nothing to those whose employers don't offer pension plans. There are no simple solutions to this dilemma, although the RRSP comes close. It is the most popular tax shelter available to Canadians, and its popularity has grown since the concept was introduced in 1957 especially among those who won't have the benefit of private pension plan payments when they retire.

With an RRSP you can set aside, untaxed, a limited amount of earnings each year. Any income earned within an RRSP is allowed to grow untaxed until withdrawn from the plan. In effect, retirement savings through an RRSP grow much quicker than those that are taxed. And when it comes time to withdraw funds from the plan the taxman will likely take a smaller cut because your overall retirement income, and marginal tax rates, will be lower.

Most people invest in off-the-shelf RRSPs offered by banks, trust companies, credit unions, insurance companies and mutual fund distributors. Others use self-directed plans through which they choose their own investments. In effect, there are two types of plans: those that pay a guaranteed rate of return and those whose returns can't be determined in advance because funds are invested in marketable securities with fluctuating prices.

But before you get carried away with plans to invest in RRSPs, you should note that there are contribution limits. For 1988 and 1989, the yearly limit is 20% of earned income up to $7,500 if you are not a member of a pension plan to which an employer makes contributions. If you are a member of such a plan, your yearly contribution for 1988 and 1989 is limited to 20% of earned income up $3,500, minus whatever you contribute to the pension plan.

These rules are about to change dramatically. The contribution limit for 1990 will increase to 18% of 1989 earned income up to a maximum of $10,500. In 1991 it will rise to $11,500 and in subsequent years will rise by $1,000 annually until it hits $15,500 in 1995. These limits will be reduced by what the federal government refers to as a "pension adjustment." This adjustment includes any contributions made to a pension plan or other tax-assisted retirement plan such as a deferred profit sharing plan. In addition, RRSP limits for those who have left a pension plan or who have made past-service contributions to their pension plans will be subject to adjustments.

In the future, calculations for RRSP contributions will be more complicated than in the past. However, employers must file pertinent information about pension contributions to the federal government, which will then calculate how much you can contribute to your RRSPs.

For 1988, you must make your your contributions no later than February 29, 1989. After that date, any unused portion of the year's limit is lost forever. But beginning in 1990 you will be allowed to carry unused contributions forward for seven years.

Cashing in

You must dispose of your RRSPs by the end of the year in which you turn 71. You have three basic options when that time comes (or before, if you wish). You can cash in your plan and pay tax on the entire amount, you can purchase an annuity, or you can put your money into a registered retirement income fund. Most people choose an RRIF (pronounced "riff"), a life annuity or some combination of the two.

Life annuities, available from life insurance companies, provide monthly income for life. But there are variations on the standard annuity. With some, payments stop when you die even if only one payment has been made. A more popular option is an annuity that pays for a guaranteed period of 10 to 15 years and until both spouses die.

Annuities pay specified rates of return that depend on your age (or your spouse's age) when you purchase the annuity. Rates also depend on general interest rates and on competition among insurance companies selling the products. Although you will receive a higher income if you take out an annuity when interest rates are high, you really have little control over timing.

Many people shy away from annuities because they involve surrendering control of assets. RRIFs, on the other hand, allow you to hold the same types of assets that are allowed in RRSPs, so investors never relinquish control. The difference between an RRSP and RRIF is that, instead of contributing assets, you withdraw funds through an RRIF.

You can withdraw as much as you like each year, which allows you to tailor your retirement income to your needs. There is a minimum RRIF withdrawal requirement, however, the fraction you arrive at when you divide one by the number of years until you or your spouse reach age 90. In other words, if you are 70 years old, you must withdraw 1/20th of the amount in your RRIF. At age 71, you would be required to withdraw 1/19th; at age 72 you must take out 1/18th; and so on. Therefore, if you were 70 years old and had $100,000 in your RRIF, you would have to withdraw at least $5,000. If your minimum withdrawal is based on the age of a younger spouse, the amount will be less.

Saving for children's education

Many families decide that the best way to save for children's education is to start a savings plan at birth. Others decide the smartest course is to pay off the mortgage as quickly as possible and finance children's education out of cash flow.

A savings plan from birth, or from when children are young, makes a great deal of sense. But the way you do it has a significant bearing on how much you'll have accumulated by the time you pack your kids off to university or another post-secondary institution. First, you should establish a separate bank or trust company account in your child's name. This should be used only for family allowance cheques, which should be deposited directly. If you have more than one child, your bank will show you how to divide the cheque among two or more accounts. But whatever you do, make sure the money goes directly into the children's accounts and not into yours.

Family allowance cheques are taxable in a parent's hands. However, if the money is invested directly on the child's behalf, any income earned on the original contribution is considered the child's. Because a child can have income in excess of $3,000 annually before your ability to use the child as a tax deduction is diminished, there is little likelihood taxes will be paid on income generated from family allowance contributions.

And remember, there is no need to leave the money in a savings account. You can invest it in Canada Savings Bonds, GICs, stocks, mutual funds and other financial instrumentsas long as your purchases are made directly from the child's account. Most people tend to use interest income investments because they are low risk or risk free.

Registered educational savings plans

There are also tax-assisted plans whereby you can save for children's education. Known as registered educational saving plans (RESPs) they allow tax-free growth of income from contributions to finance post-secondary education. The capital originally contributed is not deductible from income for tax purposes nor taxable when withdrawn, but income earned on that capital grows free of tax in the RESP until withdrawn to finance a child's education, at which time it is taxed in the beneficiary's hands. The advantage here is that students generally have low income, so the tax burden is either non-existent or negligible.

There are two variations of the RESP, both of which have distinct advantages and disadvantages.

One is the so-called "scholarship plan." In effect, your money is pooled with the funds contributed by others. The income earned in the plan is then distributed to beneficiaries the children who embark on post-secondary education. If your child decides against continuing his or her education, you get your capital back, but you forfeit any income earned. In other words, you are gambling that your child will attend a post-secondary institution. Scholarship plans are available directly from firms that sponsor them.

Portfolio-type RESPs, which allow you to choose your own investments, are offered by some brokerage houses, mutual fund companies and insurance companies. They allow parents and others to invest up to $30,000 per beneficiary, with the option of withdrawing the capital at any time. The income earned grows untaxed until withdrawn by the beneficiary to finance post-secondary education.

If the child does not go on to college or university, these plans usually allow you to change beneficiaries. You can even use the money yourself if you decide to return to school. Alternatively, you can donate the money to a recognized post-secondary institution, although the donation will not be deductible for income tax purposes.

One important point to consider about this type of RESP is the taxation of proceeds in the beneficiary's hands. All income is taxable without the benefit of associated tax breaks for interest, dividends or capital gains.

As an alternative, you may want to set up a portfolio of growth stocks or growth mutual funds for your children. While any interest or dividend income earned would be taxable in your hands, assuming you contributed the capital, any capital gains would be taxed in the children's hands. If the taxable portion exceeded the more than $3,000 each child can earn before cutting into your ability to claim that child as a tax deduction or credit, it could be applied against his or her lifetime capital gains exemption.

CHAPTER SIX

AS SAFE AS MONEY IN THE BANK

WHILE HOUSING IS CLEARLY THE FAVORITE INVESTMENT OF CANADIANS, money in the bank (or trust company or credit union) is a close second, with hundreds of billions of dollars invested in savings accounts, chequing accounts, term deposits and guaranteed investment certificates.

The volatility of interest rates during the late 1970s and early 1980s made most people sensitive to small differences in interest rates. As a result, competition among financial institutions for savings increased and an array of savings instruments became available. No longer do you have a simple choice of just two accounts – savings and chequing. Now you can choose accounts to meet your specific needs and cash flow.

Take your chequing account as an example. Traditionally, a chequing account was used just for writing cheques. You transferred enough money into it each month to cover the cheques you wrote and you neither expected nor received interest. Now it's a different story. You can find chequing accounts that pay interest, provided you maintain a minimum monthly balance. You can find chequing accounts that charge no fees, provided you maintain a minimum monthly balance. You can even get accounts that allow you to pay your bills at the bank without charge, provided you've paid an annual fee. Generally, this last type of account is part of a package that includes a personal line of credit and a credit card named after a precious metal.

Savings accounts have also come a long way. Some pay a low interest rate on the minimum outstanding balance but allow chequing privileges. However, most people who use accounts strictly for savings opt for premium savings accounts that don't allow chequing but pay a higher interest rate.

The type of premium savings account you choose depends largely on your cash flow needs. Some accounts pay interest on the minimum monthly balance, so if you keep $1,000 in your account for 29 days of one month and let the balance drop to $1 on the 30th day, you get interest for the month on only $1. Others base payments on the minimum daily balance, so if the balance in your account fluctuates widely the premium daily interest account makes more sense.

In addition, you can keep your money in term deposits with a bank or in guaranteed investment certificates with a trust company. With these you tie up your money for a specified period, which can be 30, 60, 90 or 180 days, or one year to five years.

The rates paid on term deposits and GICs generally are higher than the rates paid on savings accounts. How much higher depends on the amount you deposit and the length of time you are willing to invest. With a term deposit or GIC you agree to commit your funds for a specific time period at a specific rate. If you need your money before the end of the term you will face interest penalties in some cases. In other cases you may have to sell your GIC at a price that will reflect current interest rates.

Sometimes the best arrangement for conserving interest is to borrow against a term deposit, GIC or bank account. Let's assume you have $15,000 in an account that pays a premium rate of interest on your minimum monthly balance and you need your money before the end of the month. It will save you a few dollars if you borrow the necessary funds for several days. A pre-arranged bank credit line is the easiest loan source, but if you don't have one see your bank or trust company manager about a loan. Because you're putting up your account as collateral you should have no difficulty. And if the bank is reluctant to give you the loan or wants to charge you fees, argue the point. Banks are in business to make money and branch managers are well aware that they lose if you move your money elsewhere.

In many cases the rate paid by an institution on a longer-term deposit applies to the principal only. Interest earned on interest may be at the institution's deposit rate. Also, make sure you are comparing apples with apples. A 10% rate compounded semi-annually means you are earning 5% interest, or $50, on $1,000 for six months and 5% interest, or $52.50, on $1,050 for the next six months. This makes for a total over one year of $102.50, or an effective interest rate of 10.25%.

Table X on the next page, compares semi-annual and annual compounding of $1,000 over 10 years.

Table X

Value of $1,000 in 10 years compounded

Rate	Annually	Rate	Semi-Annually
8.00%	$2,159	7.75%	$2,139
10.00%	2,594	9.75%	2,591
12.00%	3,106	11.75%	3,132
14.00%	3,707	13.75%	3,780
16.00%	4,411	15.75%	4,554

Deciding on terms

The major investment decision facing many people who keep money on deposit is what term to take. It's not an easy choice, given the volatility of interest rates. If you lock in your money for five years at 10%, and rates move up to 17% two years later (the rate reached in mid-1982), you're out of luck; you will continue to get 10%. Conversely, people who left their money in non-chequing savings accounts at 19% in mid-1982, expecting rates to move higher, saw their returns drop below 10% within a year and to less than 7% within two years.

In effect, you have to choose between buying something like a five-year certificate at the going rate or holding off and buying a short-term certificate because you expect five-year rates to move higher. There is no reliable way to forecast such moves, particularly over the longer term. But there are some rules of thumb governing what constitutes a reasonable rate of return.

The risk-free rate, – "risk free" meaning there is no risk to capital (as is the case with an insured deposit or a government guarantee) – is generally considered to be 3% above the rate of inflation. So if you think inflation is going to be 5% over the next few years, then 8% is a reasonable rate of return. Five-year GIC rates, which in mid-1988 were about 10%, reflect an expectation that inflation may move higher. If GIC rates are below the inflation-adjusted rate of return, you are probably better off sticking to short-term deposits or savings and waiting for higher longer-term rates. For example, if five-year GICs are paying 10% and you expect 8% inflation, keep your money in 30-day or other short-term deposits until longer rates move higher or until you are satisfied that inflation is abating.

Conversely, if five-year rates are at 10% and you expect an economic slowdown, you might want to lock in the longer-term rate. That's because interest rates generally decline when the economy slows or goes into recession.

Sometimes short-term rates move higher than long-term rates. This reflects the market's view that long-term interest rates will move lower. To attract short-term money and discourage investors from investing for the long term, deposit-taking institutions raise short-term rates.

If you move into the short end of the market because you expect rates to move up and intend to switch later to five-year deposits, remember that you are speculating. Central bank interest rate policies can change overnight and you could find long-term rates moving lower than you expected. (Central banks such as the Bank of Canada are responsible for setting interest rate policies.)

If you prefer short-term savings instruments, don't overlook treasury bills or money-market mutual funds. With a money-market fund – a mutual fund that invests primarily in treasury bills and wholesale bank deposits or top quality commercial paper – you can expect to earn about two percentage points more than you would with a non-chequing savings account. So if the savings account is paying 5.75%, you would expect to earn 7.75% to 8%. Treasury bills pay even more and are at least as safe as deposits. However, the bills are usually acquired through securities dealers that charge a commission and require a minimum investment of at least $5,000. Accordingly, you should compare the net interest you would receive after commissions with the savings rate or yield available on a money-market fund. The net rate on a treasury bill is almost always higher than savings rates of comparable maturities (assuming equal investments).

Whether a treasury bill pays a superior yield to a money-market fund depends on the amount of the investment and the commission rate charged by the investment dealer. Banks also sell treasury bills, although the commissions or service fees may prove a great deal higher than those charged by investment dealers. It pays to shop around.

Deposit insurance

Money kept on deposit with a bank or trust company is covered by the Canada Deposit Insurance Corp. (credit unions have a similar insurance system). The CDIC insures each depositor for up to $60,000 in principal and interest at a specific member institution, and it is compulsory for banks and trust companies that accept deposits to belong.

The $60,000 limit cannot be circumvented by having two accounts at different branches of the same bank. However, if you have one account for yourself and another joint account with your spouse, each account is insured up to $60,000. If you have several accounts in trust for each of your children, each account is insured separately because each has a different beneficiary. Your RRSP, if on deposit with a member institution, is insured separately.

Deposit insurance applies to accounts that mature within five years and are denominated in Canadian dollars. Principal and interest are insured up to the date a claim is paid. Therefore, if you have a five-year GIC with an institution that fails before the term is up, you get your money back, plus interest owed up to the date paid. The CDIC insures your deposit, but it does not guarantee an interest rate for the term of the deposit. If you have to reinvest your funds at a lower rate than the rate on the deposit that failed, you lose the difference.

To avoid difficulties, many people choose to invest only with the largest, strongest financial institutions. Large investors such as mutual funds and pension funds may place millions of dollars with a single institution, but they carefully monitor the financial statements of that institution. If you plan to invest more than the amount covered by deposit insurance with any institution other than the major chartered banks or the largest trust companies, do your homework. And while the largest banks may have their problems with Third World debt and oil loans, it is a fair assumption that regulatory bodies would never allow them to fail under any circumstances.

You should also be aware that deposit insurance covers only deposits. It does not cover securities, such as mutual funds, which are sold by a bank or trust company. Similarly, deposit insurance doesn't cover the mortgage debentures issued by some of the largest chartered banks. They are fully guaranteed by the issuing bank, and that's generally good enough for even the most conservative investor. Otherwise, it's caveat emptor.

The whole area of investor protection is currently being studied by various regulatory bodies. In the years ahead we will likely see arrangements that raise the limits of deposit insurance, provisions for payment of benefits if a life insurance company fails, and a better system than currently exists for protecting clients of an investment dealer that runs into financial trouble.

CHAPTER SEVEN

MARKETABLE DEBT SECURITIES

MOST PERSONAL INVESTMENTS ARE IN DEBT SECURITIES. THESE GIVE the lender or investor priority in receiving payments should the borrower go broke (although some lenders get priority over others). Virtually all the savings instruments discussed in the last chapter are debt obligations of trust companies, banks and other financial institutions. Most are insured up to the limit of deposit insurance or issued by the strongest financial institutions. As a result, most of them can be considered risk free.

This chapter deals with a different kind of debt security – the type that is marketed through investment dealers and traded in the marketplace. Included in this category are instruments such as treasury bills, bonds and debentures.

The major attraction of this type of debt security is its marketability. Given the volatility of interest rates over the past two decades, many investors have decided it is worth opting for a slightly lower rate of return than might be available from a GIC in order to secure the ability to sell their investment at any time. If their investments remain liquid, they can move into shorter-term investments such as treasury bills if they feel interest rates will move higher. And if they see rates moving lower they can buy long-term bonds to lock in what they feel will prove to be a high return.

Your guarantee

Before investing in marketable debt securities it is helpful to know that there are two basic types: those guaranteed by the federal government and those that are not. Individual investors should generally stick to Government of Canada bonds for two reasons. First and foremost, they are backed by Ottawa, so your money is not at risk. Secondly, they are the most marketable bonds available in Canada. That means, as is the case with most highly marketable securities, that Government of Canada bonds have very narrow spreads between the buying price and selling price. The difference between the bid and prices for $1,000 worth of Government of Canada bonds might be as little as $5. In contrast, if you hold a corporate issue that is not actively traded the spread could be as much as $50 per $1,000.

Provincial bonds can be considered risk free as well, as can any other bonds guaranteed by federal or provincial governments. However, the spreads on these can be wider than those on Government of Canada bonds.

Corporate bonds

Corporate bonds also carry little risk at the time of issue. But a lot can happen to companies over 20 years, so unless you have a large, diversified bond portfolio and are willing to monitor the quality of your holdings frequently, once again stick to Government of Canada issues. If you decide to invest in corporate bonds because of their higher interest rates, try to stick to larger issues. (The difference in rates reflects the bonds' quality; lower-quality, higher-risk bonds pay more interest.) The prices of thinly traded bonds are usually more volatile than those of larger, broadly traded issues. You may pay less for thinly traded bonds when buying, and you may get more when selling if someone wants them desperately enough. But with a thinly traded bond issue, the selling price is often low.

If you buy corporate bonds or debentures (bonds are generally secured by specific assets, while debentures are often secured only by the general credit of the issuer) you may have a problem if a company runs into financial difficulty, even if your debt is secured. Your money could be tied up indefinitely, and the eventual settlement may not be to your liking.

Aside from the risk of default, which you can eliminate by sticking to Government of Canada bonds, there is interest rate risk. When rates rise, bond prices fall. That's because an investor wishing to buy a bond at current rates will consider an older bond with a lower rate only if the price is discounted to make the yields comparable. As Table XI on page 55 shows, rates and prices can swing widely over time.

Government bonds

The federal government raises funds by issuing three types of instruments: Canada Savings Bonds, treasury bills and marketable bonds.

A Canada Savings Bond is effectively a flexible term deposit with the government. The term of the bonds is seven years, with a fixed interest

Table XI

Monthly prices and yields of $1,000 8.5% Government of Canada bonds maturing June 1, 2011 for the period March, 1987 to April, 1988

Month	Price	% Yield
1987		
March	$980.60	8.59
April	910.60	9.45
May	906.30	9.50
June	904.40	9.52
July	867.50	10.23
August	851.30	10.17
September	795.00	10.94
October	863.10	10.02
November	839.40	10.33
December	855.00	10.13
1988		
January	900.00	9.58
February	917.50	9.38
March	875.00	9.88
April	857.50	10.10

rate for a one-year period, based on market conditions. The rate is adjusted each year, although a minimum is guaranteed for the full term. The bonds can be cashed at any time at full face value plus interest earned to the end of the previous month (with the exception of the first two months).

There are two types of Canada Savings Bonds: those that pay interest annually and compound interest bonds whereby interest is reinvested. If you buy compound bonds, remember you must declare the earned interest for income tax purposes even if you haven't received it. You can declare this interest in the year earned or allow it to compound for three years before declaring it.

Treasury bills and marketable bonds differ from savings bonds in that they are not redeemable on demand. But they can be sold through an investment dealer or bank in the active bond market. Treasury bills are short-term instruments that mature in 91 to 180 days. They are denominated in amounts of $1,000 (although the fees you would pay on a $1,000 purchase would reduce your return sharply) and sold at a discount to face value. For example, an investor purchasing a treasury bill with 60 days to maturity at $984.24 would earn an annual interest rate of 10%. In addition to federal government treasury bills, there are provincial bills that sell at slightly higher yields, reflecting a moderately larger risk.

The commercial paper chase

Major corporations and finance companies issue commercial paper similar to treasury bills in that they mature within one year and are sold at a discount to face value. Yields on commercial paper, even for very sound companies, are higher than for either federal or provincial treasury bills. For instance, 91-day treasury bills were yielding 9.21% in mid-1988, while top quality 90-day commercial paper was yielding 9.35%. The higher yields may appeal to large investors who monitor the financial strength of borrowers, but most individuals should stay out of this market. Commercial paper is usually subordinated debt, which means that if the company goes belly up, holders of the notes are paid only after secured creditors get their share.

Some companies issue commercial paper that is guaranteed by a bank. This allows small firms to tap this market for short-term funds. The rates paid reflect the quality of the guarantor.

Lower quality, high yielding commercial paper is also available. But be careful. Hundreds of millions of dollars were lost in the 1960s, when Atlantic Acceptance collapsed and its short-term paper became worthless.

Many issues of commercial paper and long-term bonds are rated by Canada's two bond rating services, Dominion Bond Rating Service of Toronto and Canadian Bond Rating Service of Montreal. In addition Moody's Investor Service Inc. and Standard and Poor's Corp., both of the U.S., rate issues of interest to U.S. investors. If you want to invest in commercial paper, stick to top quality issues only – those in the top two or three grades of rating classification. All major investment dealers selling commercial paper can supply information on ratings.

Bonds and coupon rates

Bonds issued by governments and corporations have coupon interest rates, which when multiplied by $1,000 (the usual maturity value of a bond), tell you the amount of interest paid each year. Payments are usually made semi-annually. For example, the Government of Canada bond maturing June 1, 2010, has a 9.5% coupon, which means it pays $95 interest annually with two payments of $47.50 each. However, the coupon rate does not necessarily indicate the actual return an investor will receive. In mid-1988 this bond was trading at $943.75. Because of this discount, a buyer would earn a return if the bond were held to maturity of almost

10.2% – made up of interest, plus capital appreciation of $66.25, which represents the difference between the price paid and the maturity value.

There are a number of subtle differences in the rates of return an investor would earn on two bonds issued by the same source and with identical maturity dates but different coupon rates. For example, a government bond with an 8.75% coupon and maturing in 2002 recently traded at about $890 to yield 10.24%. A 15.75% bond was trading at about $1,330 to yield 10.82%. The buyer of the discount bond would accept a lower yield because of the future capital gain. Remember, he will get back $1,000 – and while interest income is fully taxable, capital gains are only partially taxed. Therefore, the lower-coupon bond is more valuable, which makes its yield lower and its price higher.

Investors who expect interest rates to decline will often seek out discount bonds. Someone who bought that 8.75% bond and then saw interest rates decline to 8.75% from the 10% range would make a capital gain of $110 on each bond. The capital gains effect on low-coupon bonds tends to make their prices more volatile than those of bonds with higher coupons. When interest rates fall, all bond prices rise; conversely, when rates rise, bond prices fall. However, a low-coupon bond's price will rise more sharply on falling rates, and drop more precipitously on rising rates, than will the price of a high-coupon bond. The reason lies in the overall income stream of the bond.

A decline in rates increases the ultimate maturity value of the bond more than it increases the value of the interest payments. For example, $10 in interest next year is worth $9.09 today when the interest rate is 10%. And $1,000 of maturity value 10 years from now is worth $385.54 today. If interest rates drop to 5%, the present value of the interest payment will rise to $9.52, an increase of about 4.8%. But the present value of the bond's worth at maturity will shoot up to $613.91, an increase of almost 60%. With a low-coupon bond, most of the present value is in the maturity value, so an increase in interest rates magnifies the value of the capital gain, which is taxed more lightly than interest income, and pushes up low-coupon bond prices sharply. The opposite occurs when interest rates fall and capital gains shrink.

For those who want to take the risky path of speculating on interest rates, choosing bonds by the size of coupon is one possibility. If you believe interest rates are going to fall sharply in a short period, the best bonds to buy are long-term, low-coupon bonds; they will appreciate most. Conversely, if you want to hold bonds but are worried about an interest rate increase, choose high-coupon bonds over low-coupon bonds and pick a short maturity rather than a long maturity. (You can also use options

Table XII			
Change in price between two 12.5% bonds			
Bond	Price March 25, 1987	Price May 11, 1988	% change
12.5% Feb. 1, 1991	114.125	106.500	- 6.7
12.5% March 1, 2006	128.500	115.125	-10.4

and futures to speculate on or hedge against interest rate moves. These are covered in later chapters.)

Bond speculators should be aware of the effect of the term to maturity on bond prices. Long-term bonds respond more strongly to interest rate changes than do short-term bonds. The reason stems from compound interest; interest rate changes have a greater impact on payments far in the future than on payments in the near future.

Government of Canada bonds provide a real-life example of this phenomenon. Table XII shows the change in price between two 12.5% bonds. The first is relatively short-term, maturing on Feb. 1, 1991. The second matures March 1, 2006. Bond prices are quoted in points, so a bond quoted at 114.125 means it is trading at $1,141.25 per $1,000 of face value.

Just as longer-term bonds generally fall more than shorter-term bonds when interest rates rise, they gain more when interest rates fall. At the end of September 1987, the 1991 bonds were trading at $104.25. At the end of October, after the Bank of Canada lowered interest rates in response to the stock market crash, the bonds traded at $107. Over the same month, the 2006 bonds rose from $108.625 to $116.25.

One thing certain

One thing is certain: few investors can accurately predict interest rate movements. And those who are in the game for the long haul should hold bonds with a mixture of coupon rates and terms to maturity, slanting the portfolio in the direction they believe will provide the greatest short-term returns. This reflects an investment-portfolio approach to interest rate risk, with parts of the portfolio geared to generating satisfactory performance, no matter what happens to interest rates. Or you can invest in a bond mutual fund, which offers the advantages of professional management and a diversified portfolio.

If you prefer your own portfolio, there are other bond features to be considered. For example, government bonds are almost always non-callable, which means that when you buy a 20-year bond it will be outstanding for the full 20 years. That isn't the case with corporate bonds; often a corporate bond has what is known as a call feature, whereby the company issuing the bonds has the right to buy them back at a specified price after a specific number of years. If you buy a bond with a call feature, the price you pay is often based on the call date, rather than the maturity date.

Similarly, many corporate bonds have a sinking fund provision that requires a portion of the bonds to be repurchased each year after a specified number of years. The purpose of a sinking fund is to retire a number of bonds each year to reflect the depreciated value of the asset originally financed by the bonds. A sinking fund provision protects investors, and the expected diminishing supply of bonds can lead to premium prices.

In periods of rising interest rates, it is common to see issues of redeemable and extendible bonds. For example, a government might issue a 20-year bond, redeemable after five years. If you bought one of these bonds you would have the option, just before the five-year period, of keeping the bond or redeeming it for the full face value. If interest rates were higher than the coupon rate, you would likely cash in the bond and reinvest your money elsewhere. The market price of a redeemable bond would be based on the redemption date if market rates were higher than the coupon rate, and on the maturity date if market interest rates were lower than the coupon rate. An extendible bond might be issued for five years with a feature extending it, at the holder's choice, to 15 years.

Both redeemable and extendible bonds appeal to investors who are concerned that interest rates might skyrocket. Without such features governments would have difficulty attracting long-term money in periods of rising interest rates.

Some corporate debentures are convertible into common stock. The issuer may have one of two reasons for offering such debentures: to make the bonds more attractive; or to use the bonds to issue equity in a period when the market is nervous about accepting new share issues.

Convertible debentures carry coupons like those of regular debentures, although the interest rates paid would likely be lower than those paid on regular debentures. The lower coupon rate is offset by the provision that allows investors to convert their bonds to common stock at a predetermined price for a specified time period – usually several years. This way the buyer knows that if the stock price goes up, he can convert the debenture and realize a capital gain. If the stock price doesn't rise, he continues to receive interest until maturity, at which time the principal would be repaid.

The price of a convertible debenture depends on the conversion price relative to the price of the underlying stock. If a $1,000 debenture is convertible into 100 shares and the stock is selling at $15 the debenture would likely trade around $1,500. If the stock fell to $8, the convertible debenture would trade at the higher of $800 (plus some premium to reflect the possibility that the stock price might rise) or the price a debenture would trade based on its coupon rate. Most companies issuing convertible debentures, as well as the investors who buy them, hope that the price of the company's shares will rise so the debentures can be converted to stock.

Another type of bond is the so-called "junk bond," which may yield several points more than other corporate issues. The ability of a company to make the interest payments on these bonds is often questionable and the assets involved often leave little cushion for safety. That's why a buyer may get several points of interest more than, for example, a utility bond. Investors buy junk bonds because of their high coupon rates and because the market will reduce the risk premium paid and the bonds will appreciate in value if the company's profitability improves.

Some junk bonds trade at deep discounts when the issuer is in financial trouble and cannot pay the interest. These, too, offer buyers a chance at making healthy gains. Normally if a company defaults on interest, the trustee involved in the receivership will try to get its hands on company assets, and the firm is liquidated – making bonds worth much less than their original value. However, there often is another solution that benefits everyone involved, including the holders of junk bonds. All parties may agree to a settlement that will see creditors get more than they would if the company were liquidated. Bondholders speculating on this outcome between the company and its creditors find their bonds are suddenly worth a great deal more because their share of assets increased.

Where to buy

Where do you buy bonds? In Canada, they trade "over-the-counter," rather than on a stock-market type of exchange. This means you buy and sell bonds through an investment dealer and banks. Most knowledgeable traders deal with investment dealers because the costs are less and the returns are higher. Both investment dealers and banks will sell new government issues at the issued price, without commission.

A dealer with a bond department is most likely buying bonds as principal, which means the dealer will buy bonds at one price from you and sell them at a higher price to another investor (or hold them in inventory). If a dealer buys as principal, its fee is built into the price paid and no additional commission is payable. Similarly, if you sell a bond, the price received from the dealer would include the dealer's markup.

Some investment dealers don't have bond departments. If you deal with this type of institution, it will likely purchase from or sell to another dealer. In this case, your dealer will tack on a commission. It is best, however, to work with a dealer that has a specialized bond department with expert staff. But remember, bond trading is a big business, so don't expect much service if you're trading only a few thousand dollars worth of bonds.

CHAPTER EIGHT

PREFERRED SHARES: THE 'BOND STOCK'

A PREFERRED SHARE CAN BE VIEWED AS A BOND THAT HASN'T QUITE made it in terms of safety, or as a common stock without the profit potential. Investors buy preferred shares because they pay dividends that, because of the dividend income-tax credit, generally pay an after-tax rate of return greater than that of interest-paying investments such as bonds and GICs.

As noted in the chapter on taxation of investment income, the rule of thumb is that $1 of dividend income from a Canadian corporation is equal on an after-tax basis to $1.26 of interest income. So if your choice is between a bond with a yield of 10% and a preferred share yielding a little more than 8%, the preferred will return more. But there are other considerations, such as the safety of your investment. Many people would rather take a slightly lower return on a guaranteed investment and worry less. However, when properly chosen, preferreds have a definite advantage over interest-paying securities because of that higher after-tax return. (You would not include preferred shares in your RRSP for income because an RRSP cannot take advantage of the dividend tax credit.)

Preferred shareholders are, in fact, owners of the company. But they generally don't have a vote on company affairs – a privilege usually reserved for common shareholders. Still, preferred shares have more clout when it comes to dividends; preferred shareholders get their share of company profits before common shareholders (after interest due on bonds and other debt securities is paid).

If a company fails, preferred shareholders are entitled to nothing until all creditors, including bondholders, are paid. But preferred shareholders take precedence over common shareholders when a company winds up. Yet this may be of little comfort because companies that go under usually have a liquidation value that is too low to repay even the creditors. In addition, preferred shareholders have somewhat less protection in the event of a takeover than do common shareholders.

Preferred dividends are usually fixed, either in dollars or as a percentage of par (nominal) value. For example, a glance at Toronto Stock Exchange stock tables shows at least five British Columbia Telephone Co. preferred issues, each paying different percentages. On the other hand, BCE Inc. preferred shares include annual dividends in dollars and cents.

When earnings are inadequate, the preferred dividend will be skipped. But most preferred share issues have a cumulative feature requiring that all preferred dividends be paid, including those in arrears, before any common stock dividend is declared.

Even though preferred stock issues are safer than common, company failure or dividend default should be a concern. If you are buying preferred shares for income, you should consider only those issued by financially solid companies. The same services that rate commercial paper and bonds also rate preferred shares, so inform your broker the only preferreds you wish to consider are those with P1 and P2 ratings – the two highest classifications. And make sure your broker informs you of any changes in the ratings of your stock.

In addition to sticking to the strongest companies, diversify your holdings in case one of your investments turns sour. If the fortunes of a company in which you hold preferreds become clouded, you are probably better off selling. The adage that your first losses are your smallest often proves true.

The preferred market can seem complicated for the novice because of the different types of shares available. What they have in common – at least when issued by major companies – is that they trade on stock exchanges, just like common stocks. The following are some of the types of preferred shares available:

Straight Preferreds: These do not carry a maturity date and are, in effect, a perpetual security. Prices of straight preferreds are most sensitive to changes in interest rates. They can be volatile in periods of sharply changing rates, but are extremely attractive in periods of high rates – particularly if it appears that rates will fall.

Retractable Preferreds: These give the holder the right to redeem the shares at a specific date for par value. This is an attractive provision because it protects investors against a sharp increase in interest rates. Retractable preferreds are a good choice in periods when the direction of rates is uncertain.

Floating-rate Preferreds: These have an interest rate that floats with changes in the prime rate. Floating-rate preferreds are the best bet during periods of rising interest rates.

Convertible Preferreds: These are convertible into common stock. Convertibles, particularly those issued by utilities, are popular with those who invest for income. In the short term, the convertible preferred pays a higher dividend than the common share. But in the longer term, there is a high probability that the common dividend will increase to a point that exceeds the preferred dividend. At that point investors would convert their convertible preferreds to common shares.

The fact that preferred dividends are more certain than common stock dividends is a big plus for investors who want to maximize after-tax income. Even so, not every investor holds preferreds for income. Some buy those with dividends in arrears as speculative investments, hoping for capital gains if the company pays past dividends. But whatever the reason for investing, don't lose sight of the fact that shares of any sort are not as safe as government bonds. As a result, you must monitor your holdings carefully. Or if you're not prepared to take that route, consider investing in preferreds through a mutual fund whose professional manager will decide on what stocks have the best potential.

CHAPTER NINE

COMMON STOCKS: THE INSIDE STORY

TO MANY PEOPLE IT ISN'T THAT IMPORTANT WHETHER GAMBLING IS legalized in Canada. After all, they can always take a chance on the stock market.

But stocks don't have to be a gamble. Thousands of individual and institutional investors who play the stock markets are rewarded with long-term profits far above what they would earn in guaranteed investments and bonds. However, to be successful you must know how the markets work.

Stock price movements on organized Canadian exchanges – the Toronto Stock Exchange, the Montreal Exchange, the Vancouver Stock Exchange and the Alberta Stock Exchange – and on the major American exchanges are continuously reported and updated during each trading day. With the exception of the Alberta exchange, the exchanges publish indexes of price movements that chronicle the aggregate ups and downs of the market.

Common shares, which represent ownership of a company, constitute by far the largest portion of listed stocks. Prices of common shares may change throughout each trading day. Share prices reflect the general outlook for the stock market; investor expectations about a firm's profits, dividends and other developments that affect the company; and the prospects for the industry the firm is involved in. Common share prices are generally much more volatile than prices of bonds or preferred shares, and some stocks are more erratic than others. For example, shares of a telephone utility that pays a high dividend will be more stable than a those of a penny mine with unknown prospects and whose share price reflects speculators' expectations.

Stock markets move in cycles, with prices rising and falling in response to changing investor expectations. However, if you have a diversified portfolio of stocks and hold them for some time, you can expect to earn a rate of return several percentage points higher than if you invest in guaranteed investments.

Some investors choose to invest in only a single stock or a small number of stocks in the hope of quickly making a substantial profit. Some succeed, but portfolios with only a few stocks tend to be more volatile – than those of a widely diversified portfolio.

The Toronto Stock Exchange 300 composite index reflects the prices of the 300 TSE-listed stocks with the largest market capitalizations. Market capitalization is the value of the shares traded on the exchange, or the price of the shares multiplied by the number of shares outstanding. Therefore, a company with 10 million shares outstanding and a stock price of $25 has a market capitalization of $250 million.

Table XIII 12 Month % returns of TSE vs. T-Bills For Periods Ended June 30		
	TSE	T-bills
1974	-9.3	6.8
1975	9.7	7.5
1976	4.7	8.5
1977	2.6	8.2
1978	14.6	7.5
1979	49.9	10.2
1980	32.6	12.9
1981	18.8	14.8
1982	-39.1	16.5
1983	86.6	10.0
1984	-6.1	10.0
1985	26.6	10.7
1986	17.4	9.3
1987	24.6	8.0
1988	-5.2	8.7

Over the 10 years ended June 30, 1988, the TSE total return index, which is the gain in the TSE 300 index plus stock dividends, recorded an average annual compound return of 16%, almost five percentage points more than you would have earned by holding treasury bills. Table XIII, shows the year-by-year performance of the Toronto Stock Exchange total return index and the rate of return on federal treasury bills. (for periods ended June 30.) The total return index is a good representation of what you would have earned by holding a broadly based stock portfolio.

Market cycles vary in length. Rising periods are called "bull markets" and falling markets are known as "bear markets." Table XIV on the next page, compiled by Toronto statistician Richard Anstett, shows market cycles of the TSE 300 from 1919 to the present.

The October 1987 crash – when the Toronto market fell more than 22% – has to be looked at in its proper context. Between July 1982 and August 1987 the market gained 202%. In the subsequent three months it

Table XIV

Market Cycles on the Toronto Stock Exchange

Bullish Periods	no. of months	% gain	Bearish Periods	no. of months	% loss
August 1921, to September 1929	97	300	September 1929, to June 1932	33	80
June 1932, to March 1937	57	201	March 1937, to April 1942	61	56
April 1942 to May 1946	49	159	May 1946, to February 1948	21	25
February 1948, to July 1956	101	273	July 1956, to December 1957	17	30
December 1957, to May 1969	137	162	May 1969, to June 1970	13	28
June 1970, to October 1973	40	64	October 1973, to December 1974	14	38
December 1974, to November 1980	72	193	November 1980, to July 1982	20	44
July 1982, to August 1987	61	202	August 1987, to October 1987	2	31
October 1987, to July 1988	9	24	(Changes in market sentiment reflect gains or declines of 20% or more.)		

fell 31%. Investors who jumped in after the crash have done quite well, with the index gaining 24% to the end of June 1988.

Investment techniques

One technique for investing in the stock market is to put together a diversified portfolio of shares in senior companies with solid histories of earnings and good prospects for the future. This kind of diversification spreads risk among many companies. You then constantly monitor your holdings, adding new investments that appear to have better than average prospects and selling those that no longer meet your expectations. You can do this by conducting your own analysis, by depending on your broker for advice or by using professional management through a mutual fund. Some brokerage houses, investment counselling firms and trust companies also have investment management divisions that will look after your portfolio.

Another stock market investment technique, as we've already mentioned, is to hold only a few stocks in the hope of making gains far greater than those you would get from a diversified portfolio. This method suits some investors well, while others lose most of their capital. People who employ this technique specialize in trying to pick stocks before their prices start to rise and in unloading their dogs before they start to bark.

What separates the winners from the losers are their methods of picking stocks. Winners tend to use detailed analysis of companies, often confining their research to firms that are not widely followed by the investment industry in the hope of finding an undiscovered bargain. The share price of widely followed companies generally reflects all the known information, so it's difficult to stay ahead of the crowd when investing in these issues.

Benjamin Graham's legacy

The most successful method of investment analysis – perhaps at once the simplest and the most complicated – is the Benjamin Graham method, named for the American analyst who developed it more than 60 years ago. Simply put, it involves searching for value. The share price should be below the value of company assets (after deducting liabilities) each share represents. Although there are many variations of the method, including careful consideration of earnings trends and developments that may enhance a company's earnings, it all comes down to buying value.

The Benjamin Graham method is not always the most exciting way of assessing stocks. It requires patience, but it usually proves profitable over the long term. And you won't get badly burned, particularly if you remember to sell when a stock's price rises above its underlying value.

Other methods involve buying into a falling market and selling when prices are rising. However, most stock market investors find it emotionally difficult to move against the crowd. Indeed, this so-called "contrarian" approach takes a great deal more discipline than the Graham approach. Even so, a follower of Graham is more likely to be buying near the bottom and selling near the top.

Some investors play interest rate cycles. When interest rates move up sharply, stock prices usually move lower; declining interest rates are usually associated with rising stock markets. But playing interest rates can be extremely tricky. Rates can move higher because of demand for funds by growing companies, so selling on this basis can be costly in terms of potential profits.

Technical analysis is another way to predict market behavior and to choose stocks. This technique looks not at balance sheets and income statements, but at charts of market and individual stock performance, trading volumes, various ratios of advancing stocks versus declining stocks and so on. Many people are skeptical about technical analysis, yet virtually every brokerage house has a highly paid technical analyst whose job is to produce observations that individuals and brokers can consider when making investment decisions.

All shares are not equal

Investors should also be aware that there are different types of common stock, especially when it comes to voting privileges. At one time, common shareholders had one vote for each share held. This has changed in recent years and a number of companies now have two classes of common shares, one of which is a subordinated share for voting purposes. The regular common shares generally carry more votes per share than the subordinated common shares. As a result, control of the company's affairs often lies with a group of investors who have substantial voting power but less than a majority of the equity in the company.

This normally isn't a problem for investors, except when a takeover offer is made. Securities law requires that when a premium price is paid for a control block of shares (the premium must be 15% or more) a comparable offer must be made to all holders of that class of shares. This means that a takeover offer at a substantial premium to the market price will be made to the common shareholders, but not to the holders of subordinated common shares. Some companies with subordinated shares have what are called "coattail" provisions that are designed to protect holders of those shares in the event of a takeover. However the market tends to discount the price of subordinated shares, even when there is a coattail.

There have been a number of cases over the past few years in which companies have been bought out, or offers made, with better deals for the common shareholders who control the company. As a result, some institutional investors have a policy of buying only shares that control the vote, even though it means paying a premium. If you decide to invest in a company that has two classes of common shares, check how the coattail, if there is one, protects you. If you're not sure, play it safe and go for the shares that will benefit from a takeover offer.

In the end, consistent profits are made by being careful, avoiding excessive greed and doing a lot of homework. Certainly, the investor who buys a stock simply because he believes there exists a greater fool who will pay more for the stock, is often the greater – and poorest – fool.

Unfortunately, many people get their first taste of the stock market by buying the penny dreadfuls – over-the-counter stocks (stocks not traded on an exchange) sold over the telephone by dealers who are not members of any exchange and who peddle paper and prey on people's greed and dreams.

If you are interested in getting rich quickly, you must develop an expertise in a specific area of the market, most likely in natural resources, and be prepared for massive ups and downs. Big money can be made, but luck is as much a part of it as is skill. And don't forget the adage about not putting all your eggs in one basket. Speculate with only a portion of your savings that is no larger than the amount you can afford to lose without affecting your lifestyle and long-term goals.

Employee purchase plans

Many companies offer stock-purchase plans to encourage employees to become owners in their enterprises. Some plans are good; others are much better. The key points to remember are diversification: You shouldn't put everything in one stock, particularly if your industry is cyclical and you may need to cash out when the industry is the dumps. Remember, too, that such stocks are long-term investments. If you think you'll need your money in a year or so, stay out of the plan.

As part of a basic employee stock-purchase plan, the company puts up the funds for share purchases and allows the employee to pay the funds back through payroll deductions. The interest charged is generally equal to the stock dividends received and is deductible for tax purposes. A better plan involves the company matching your purchases, so you effectively get your holdings for half price. The company's purchases on your behalf are a taxable benefit.

Other companies give employees options to buy stock at a specific price for a specific time period. The advantage of the option is that you exercise it only if the stock goes up. The disadvantage is that the difference between the exercise price and market price is taxed as income, not as a capital gain.

Another variation is the option loan plan. The option is granted at some price higher than the market price of the stock. Once the share price rises above the exercise price the option is exercised and financed by a loan from the company. Any subsequent profits are capital gains.

CHAPTER TEN

MUTUAL FUNDS: SUITABLE FOR EVERYONE

FOR MANY PEOPLE, MUTUAL FUNDS (ALSO KNOWN AS INVESTMENT funds) are the best way to invest – whether it be in stocks, bonds, mortgages, treasury bills or a combination of investment vehicles.

Mutual funds are pools of capital owned by many investors who buy shares, or units, of funds. The value of each share represents the total value of the fund's investment portfolio, divided by the number of shares outstanding. Most Canadian funds are "open-ended," which means that the number of outstanding shares varies according to the number of people purchasing or redeeming shares.

The pools of capital are invested by professional fund managers in a portfolio of securities, with the types of securities purchased reflecting the fund's objectives. For example a fund whose goal is long-term growth within the framework of the Canadian economy would generally invest in common shares of Canadian companies. A fund whose objective is to earn current income might hold bonds or mortgages.

Mutual funds are extremely popular, with an estimated 1.5 million Canadians holding about $30 billion in the country's 460 mutual funds. There are several reasons for this popularity. First, mutual funds provide investors with an opportunity to diversify their investments. Because money is spread among many securities, investors are unlikely to suffer great financial losses if one investment goes sour. Most mutual funds that hold stocks own shares of at least 20 companies.

A second important reason for the popularity of mutual funds is professional management. In a mutual fund, investors' money is under the management of a full-time investment professional whose job is to select and maintain a portfolio of securities that meets the fund's objectives. Professional management often gives investors higher returns than they could earn on their own.

In addition, mutual funds offer a selection of investment opportunities that is not generally available to individuals. For example, some funds hold bonds payable in foreign currencies but issued by Canadian government agencies or corporations – instruments most individual investors simply don't have the capital to buy. Even investors who usually invest directly in securities can benefit from mutual funds, particularly if they want to invest a portion of their money in a specific market, such as Japan, and reap the rewards of diversification and professional management.

Another big plus for mutual funds is liquidity. Investors can redeem shares of most funds on any business day, and the proceeds will be in their hands within a week.

Types of funds

Mutual funds fall into two main categories: growth and income. Within these categories are a number of types of funds, ranging from those that invest in a wide range of securities to those that concentrate on sectors such as precious metals or energy stocks. Some meet Revenue Canada's Canadian content requirements for inclusion in registered retirement savings plans, while others invest internationally. Most growth funds that are eligible for RRSPs invest in a broad spectrum of Canadian common shares covering many industries, but there are also RRSP-eligible specialty funds that focus on smaller sectors of the Canadian economy. Even within the international group of funds, investors can choose specialty funds such as health funds or funds that concentrate their holdings in a single geographical area.

Fixed-income funds include bond funds, mortgage funds, preferred-share funds, money-market funds and funds that combine two or more of these investments. Almost all the bond, mortgage and money-market funds – more than 100 in total – are RRSP eligible.

Preferred-share funds invest primarily in dividend-paying preferred shares, and are usually purchased by investors who want high after-tax returns outside the shelter of an RRSP. Proceeds from such funds are eligible for the federal dividend tax credit, which effectively reduces the tax rate on dividends so that after-tax rates of return from preferred shares are competitive with those for bonds. However, the dividend tax credit cannot be used within an RRSP.

Money-market funds invest in short-term debt securities such as government treasury bills, in deposits with major financial institutions and in corporate debt. Consequently, their rates of return are stable.

Of course, some funds are involved in a number of areas. There are a number of balanced funds and managed-asset-mix funds that combine growth and income investments, with the mix of these vehicles changing according to market conditions. These have been growing in popularity since the October 1987 stock market decline, when such funds performed better than pure equity funds.

Mutual funds are available through a number of sources. Some are offered through independent mutual fund dealers and stockbrokers who deal in funds offered by several fund-management groups. Others are offered directly by their managers through affiliates or direct sales forces. Most major banks and trust companies also offer families of funds, while major insurance companies offer mutual funds or segregated funds that are similar to mutual funds.

Funds sold through a sales force are generally sold with a commission payable to the salesperson. This commission usually ranges up to 9%, with a sliding scale of reductions for larger purchases – for example, the maximum commission on a $50,000 purchase might be 5%. In addition, virtually every fund allows commissions to be negotiated, which gives brokers the latitude to adjust fees to be competitive and to reflect the level of service provided.

If you invest $1,000 in a fund and require a lot of advice, don't expect a reduction in the commission. But if you invest $50,000 and require little service or information from a financial advisor, you should be able to negotiate a lower fee.

Some funds tack on a sales charge if you redeem your shares within a specified period, although the charge often declines with the number of years the fund is held. In this case you are likely to pay a higher management fee than you would for a fund with a front-end load.

Funds sold directly by fund-management companies, as well as those sold by bank and trust companies, are generally no-load funds – meaning they are sold without a commission. With no-load funds, all your money goes to work for you. However, you are generally on your own as far as advice is concerned.

There are exceptions. Some no-load funds have staff members who offer limited advice on funds (but not detailed financial planning), and some trust companies and banks have recently improved the quality of information they provide to investors.

Fund	3 mo.	6 mo.	1 yr.	3 yr.	5 yr.	10 yr.	%	St.D.
EQUITY FUNDS – RRSP ELIGIBLE								
AGF Excel Cdn Equity Fund	5.2	3.3	–	–	–	–	N/A	–
AIC Advantage Fund	6.8	1.5	-9.2	–	–	–	N/A	–
AMD Cdn Blue Chip Growth Fd	5.8	2.1	-9.4	–	–	–	N/A	–
All-Canadian Compound Fund	1.3	2.4	-9.3	6.9	8.4	13.6	28	3.77
All-Canadian Dividend Fund	1.3	2.3	-9.3	6.8	8.1	13.3	27	3.77
Allied Canadian Fund	4.8	-2.9	-28.6	–	–	–	N/A	–
Associate Investors Ltd.	4.7	4.9	-0.3	9.6	12.9	15.7	26	3.53
Bolton Tremblay Cda Cum Fund	7.0	4.3	-7.7	6.9	6.0	13.1	46	4.26
Bolton Tremblay Cdn Balanced	3.6	2.6	–	–	–	–	N/A	–
Bolton Tremblay Discovery	2.3	0.8	–	–	–	–	N/A	–
Bullock Growth Fund	7.3	3.3	-6.0	9.6	3.6	11.2	86	5.20
CDA RSP Balanced Fund	4.0	2.5	0.5	10.6	11.1	–	6	2.07
CDA RSP Common Stock Fund	8.6	4.5	-4.9	13.6	14.1	16.2	55	4.48
CGF Fund 4000	4.0	0.9	-13.4	7.8	8.6	11.4	79	4.92
CGF Venture Fund	4.7	2.0	-20.2	-9.8	-5.7	1.9	99	6.97
CMA Investment Fund	6.1	6.1	6.1	15.5	16.1	17.8	26	3.53

The rate of return you can earn from a fund depends on the type of fund, market conditions, the length of time you hold the fund and the skills of the fund manager.

Generally speaking, funds that invest for growth provide the highest long-term rates of return – often 16% annually or more over a period of 10 to 20 years. In the short term, however, there is no way of predicting rates of return for a growth fund. Consequently, they should not be purchased with the view of making money over a very short period.

Even so, some growth funds are a lot less volatile than others. Each month, Financial Times of Canada publishes a survey of investment funds, which includes short- and long-term rates of return for about 460 funds as shown in the above table. (For a complete listing see Appendix C and D.) In addition the survey tracks the volatility of many funds through two methods. The first figure indicates the percentage of funds within a group that are more volatile than a specific fund. For example, in the RRSP-eligible growth fund list, gold funds generally have ratings in excess of 90% reflecting the fact that gold funds are among the most volatile funds available. Conversely, balanced funds which have relatively stable rates of return would be among the least volatile of the group and have ratings of less than 15%. If you want a stable rate of return, you will often have to settle for lower overall performance. And if you want certainty, the only option is a money-market fund. Because money-market funds invest in only short-term instruments, you can redeem shares at any time and collect everything you invested, plus interest. Money-market funds have historically paid about two percentage points more than premium savings accounts, but that rate of return is dwarfed by the long-term performance of growth funds. Still, money-market funds offer excellent investment potential for those with short-term savings objectives – such as a down payment on a home.

Bond funds and other income funds usually provide medium- and long-term rates of return that fall between those of money-market and growth funds. They are more volatile than money-market funds but less volatile than growth funds because the income generated by the underlying assets stabilizes returns. They are best suited to people who want current income in their portfolios or who want more stability than is available from growth funds.

Even though growth funds offer the best long-term returns, you should consider market conditions before making a purchase. If conditions suggest that stock prices are expensive, you may want to put your money elsewhere. Most equity fund managers will protect investors by building up cash reserves when stock prices seem high. But if you are nervous about market conditions you may want to choose a more conservative fund, or a mixture of fund types. You might also consider funds with a mixture of asset types – balanced or managed-asset-mix funds – that make these decisions for you. These multi-type funds are designed to invest in growth assets when they perform best and in income assets when it is prudent to do so.

Most investors buy funds entirely on the basis of performance. Undoubtedly, performance is important because it shows how a manager has performed relative to competitors under identical market conditions. But there is a pitfall: you should make sure the person responsible for those performance figures is still running the fund; if not, past performance may be misleading. A fund's volatility ranking can also provide valuable performance clues. Top-performing funds with high volatility ratings often perform poorly in down markets.

And look at a number of time periods when judging funds. It is surprising how investors' conclusions can change when judging the performance of funds over different periods.

CHAPTER ELEVEN

REAL ESTATE: PERILS AND PROBLEMS

IF YOU'RE LIKE MOST CANADIANS, THE LARGEST SINGLE INVESTMENT you'll ever make will be in real estate. As a result, the family home is likely to be your major asset. Following closely behind may be an addition to your home, or even a second residence for vacation purposes or investment gains.

Real estate has been a financial winner for thousands of Canadians in many parts of the country over the past few decades. But the road has not always been a smooth one. In some parts of the country, real estate prices have been volatile. In Alberta, for example, prices plunged a few years ago when the bottom fell out of oil prices. Some people walked away from their mortgages because they owed more than their homes were worth.

Even with regional ups and downs, the forces that have pushed prices higher in many markets remain intact. They include a sharp shift in demographics that has increased the number of young families and singles reaching home-purchasing age, as well as speculative and inflationary forces and relatively low interest rates.

Yet even with the positive history housing has had as an investment, many people choose to be renters. And for good reason – despite price increases, renting is still one of the best bargains in town. Monthly rental payments across Canada run at 50% to 75% of ownership costs.

The better paid, and presumably more sophisticated in matters of finance, are the major group owning homes. Indeed, the vast majority of high-income Canadian families own their own homes.

Are these people crazy to own instead of saving money by paying rent? More to the point, should you buy a house? Or if you are already an owner, should you sell your house and rent instead?

Part of the answer lies in where rents are headed. The vacancy rate in rental housing in most urban areas is low, which means there are few rental apartments or houses available at any given time.

High mortgage rates, inflated maintenance costs and soaring purchase prices have combined with rent controls to make the building of new rental units both unprofitable and risky. Once a building is constructed, there is no difficulty renting it out if rates are competitive with existing rent-controlled structures (except in markets with low vacancy rates, where new units rent at much higher prices). However, it is just about impossible to keep rents moving up as quickly as maintenance and financing costs. As a result, it seems unlikely that the existing rental structure will prevail. Within the next few years, unless there is general price deflation, the existing rental structure may fall apart. Alternatively, buildings will deteriorate to the point that fewer acceptable rental units will be available and new units put on the market will carry much higher rents.

Yet soaring rents do not automatically mean it will be better to own than to rent. However, as rents rise many renters will find home ownership attractive, and the subsequent demand will push up housing prices.

Whither housing prices?

If rising rents mean rising house prices, then the rationale for home ownership that has prevailed for more than two decades will continue. When monthly rental costs are lower than ownership costs, the only economic justification for owning rather than renting is the expectation that housing prices will rise. The expected price increase promises a tax-free capital gain for the homeowner, collectible when the house is sold. The value of that capital gain must offset the higher monthly ownership costs.

The promise of rising housing prices has been fulfilled in the past. In the early 1970s – a golden era for home ownership – prices soared at rates in excess of 20% a year. Over the longer run, the average annual rate of house price appreciation has been closer to 8%.

With today's low inflation rates, 8% appreciation may be higher than can be expected in the long term. Of course, specific locations can offer differing rates of appreciation. On average, however, it is unlikely that prices will rise more rapidly than the inflation rate – and that may not be enough if mortgage rates stay in the neighborhood of 10% to 11%. Does it make much sense to pay 11% interest on an investment that appreciates by only 5% annually?

If mortgage rates stay some seven or so percentage points above inflation, the results could be disastrous for homeowners. The only factors keeping house prices from dropping sharply would be expectations of rising rents and the return of higher inflation rates.

There are three crucial variables in the economics of the decision to buy a home.

The first is the amount of money needed to buy – including the down payment, financing and legal fees and renovation costs. The second is the monthly difference be-

Table XV

Excerpts from 25-year mortgage table
(Dollars are per $1,000
of original mortgage)

Rate	Monthly payment	Mortgage remaining at end of five years
12%	$10.32	$955
13%	11.02	961
14%	11.74	966

tween ownership payments and rental payments. Ownership payments include mortgage costs, taxes, property insurance and maintenance. And don't forget to include heat and other utilities as part of your rental costs if they are paid separately. The third variable is the expected price of the home at the end of the time period on which you are basing your decision, less the mortgage outstanding at that time.

In a nutshell, the difference between the third variable and the first is the increase in the value of the ownership interest. That amount must exceed the total of the second variable – the extra monthly costs of owning rather than renting – if buying a house is to make economic sense.

Let's assume a house is priced at $100,000 and requires $30,000 for a down payment, closing fees and renovations (beyond what would be undertaken with rented quarters. Let's also assume the five-year mortgage is for $75,000, amortized over 25 years at a 12% interest rate.

Table XV shows the monthly payment, as well as the mortgage remaining at the end of five years.

You can calculate that the monthly mortgage payment will be $774 (75 times $10.32) and the mortgage outstanding at the end of five years will be $71,625 (75 times $955).

If taxes and utilities are $350 a month, the monthly costs of owning are $1,124 ($774 plus $350). Now let's assume similar rental accommodation could be had for $700 a month. As a result, the net monthly cost of owning rather than renting is $424 ($1,124 minus $700).

However, a number of adjustments must be made before a valid comparison is possible. That's because the ability to earn interest on funds over time makes it incorrect to compare sums to be received, for instance, in five years with sums to be spent today.

If someone offers to sell you a promise that he will give you $1,000 in five years, the price you will be willing to pay today is considerably less than $1,000. The reason is interest. At 10% compounded annually, you need invest only $620.92 today to receive $1,000 in five years.

The problem of comparing future dollars with current dollars is common in business. Managers are always being asked to lay out money for plant and equipment today for benefits that will be received in the future. Essentially, this is exactly what a the buyer of a home is doing.

The technique used for reducing future dollars so they can be compared with current dollars is called present-value calculation. "Smart" pocket calculators have such programs, as do the spreadsheet programs used with personal computers.

| Table XVI |
| Present Value of $1 to Be Received at the End of Five Years |

Interest rate (%)	Present value ($)
2	0.906
4	0.822
6	0.747
8	0.681
10	0.621
12	0.567
14	0.519
16	0.476
18	0.437
20	0.402
22	0.370
24	0.341
26	0.315
28	0.291
30	0.269

Before the advent of these electronic marvels, we had to choose between laborious hand calculations or the use of present-value tables. Table XVI is an abbreviated example of the present-value table needed to convert a single sum in the future to its present day equivalent.

Using the table, you can see that if you invest at an after-tax rate of 14%, $80,000 in five years is worth only $41,520 today, ($80,000 times 0.519). However, if the interest rate is 10%, $80,000 in five years is worth $49,680 today ($80,000 times 0.621).

The difference in monthly payments must also be converted to a present value. Table XVII on the next page shows the present value of $1 monthly payments over five years at differing rates of interest.

Five hundred dollars a month for five years is worth $18,870 today at a 20% interest rate (500 times $37.74). At 10%, $500 a month is worth $23,535 (500 times $47.07).

What, then, is the $424 in monthly costs of owning worth? That depends on your after-tax borrowing costs. If it is 8%, the present value of $424 a month is $20,911.68 ($424 times 49.32).

This means that just to break even on owning, rather than renting, the present value of your ownership interest must increase by $20,911.68 over five years. Since your original investment was $30,000, the present value of the house must be at least $50,911.68 to justify owning ($30,000 plus $20,911.68).

As a first step in calculating the required value of the house in five years, the present value of $50,911.68 must be converted into its equivalent five years into the future. Table XVI on the previous page, indicates that $1 in five years is worth $0.681 today. So $50,911.68 today is worth $74,760.18 in five years ($50,911.68 divided by 0.681). You must then add the remainder of the mortgage in five years. The unamortized portion of a mortgage at the end of five years can be found in a book of mortgage tables.

The relevant section is shown in the third column of Table XV. At the end of five years, a mortgage of $75,000 at 12%

Table XVII

Present value of 60
monthly payments of $1

Interest rate (%)	Present value ($)
2	57.05
4	54.30
6	51.73
8	49.32
10	47.07
12	44.96
14	42.98
16	41.12
18	39.38
20	37.74
22	36.21
24	34.76
26	33.40
28	32.12
30	30.91

will be $71,625 ($955 times 75). When the remaining mortgage and the required increase in ownership interest are combined, the value of the house must be about $146,385 ($71,625 plus $74,760) in five years to justify the purchase. In other words, the house price must rise by more than 46.4% ($46,385 divided by $100,000) over five years.

We noted earlier that the long-term rate of housing price appreciation is 8% a year. Is 46.4% over five years at all close to 8%? To find out, take a look at the compound interest tables as shown in Appendix B.

The factor for our example is 1.4639 ($146,385 divided by $100,000). The required rate of house-price appreciation, then, is just a bit less than 8% annually – almost equaling the historic long-run rate of 8% a year. If we are confident the 8% rate will be achieved, the housing purchase makes sense as a break-even situation.

Of course, there is no guarantee that the future will be like the past. With low inflation, the rate of price appreciation may be less than 8%. Still, adding in the non-economic returns of home ownership, a reasonable person would probably decide to buy, based on all these numbers.

Should you sell your home?

Suppose you already own your home and you're thinking of selling now that its price has increased greatly since you bought it. Is this the time to sell and move into rental quarters, or is it better to hold on to the house and hope for further price appreciation? Determining the answer requires exactly the same analysis as was used to determine whether a home purchase makes sense. The cost of holding on to your home equals the net proceeds you would receive if you sold it. (Remember, net proceeds are the selling price, less sales commission, less paying off the mortgage balance, less any penalties that the mortgage lender may require for early payment.) You should also subtract from the price any legal fees involved in the sale and any renovation costs needed beyond what would have to be done in a similar rented facility.

Table XVIII

Annual compound interest for five years

Interest rate (%)	Value at end of 5 years divided by original cost ($)
1	1.05101
2	1.10408
3	1.15927
4	1.21665
5	1.27628
6	1.3382
7	1.4026
8	1.4693
9	1.5386
10	1.6105
11	1.6851
12	1.7623
13	1.842
14	1.925
15	2.01

The remainder of the analysis is identical to that followed by a home buyer. The monthly differences in costs between renting and owning have to be reduced to a present value, and added to the net proceeds of selling. This sum must be divided by the present value factor to determine the required increase in ownership value in five years. This, in turn, must be added to the unamortized mortgage outstanding in five years to determine the required selling price. Then the question is: How likely is it that such a price will be achieved in five years?

Using Table XVIII, the ratio of required price in five years to the forgone sales proceeds today can be translated into an annual compound growth rate. You also have to decide on how reasonable the required growth rate is, considering historic patterns and current conditions, including the probable path of inflation. Finally, youmust consider local market conditions. For instance, a market that has seen huge increases recently may stablize or even turn down.

The economics of buying a cottage as a second home involves an analysis identical to buying a first home, with one important difference: The capital gain on selling a second home may be taxable in part, depending on whether you've used your $100,000 lifetime capital gains exemption and whether your gains exceed this amount.

The exemption has undoubtedly spurred sales of country cottages. But buyers should be very careful; price appreciation of second homes does not necessarily follow the same pattern as price movements in first homes.

Population growth is a major factor in explaining the differences. Back in the 1950s and 1960s, Canada's population was surging and it moved beyond traditional city limits as city property values rose. Businesses were also moving from urban areas in search of less expensive land and lower taxes, so they pulled even more people in their wake as workers were tempted to move to the countryside to be closer to work.

In the past decade, explosive population growth has slowed, reducing the upward pressure on urban land values in some centres. Furthermore, urban areas have found themselves stuck with empty factory sites because of the combination of high land costs and high taxes. Cities are rapidly developing programs to keep and attract new businesses and jobs. These changes should result in a slowing of the movement to rural areas and, hence, a lower rate of price increase for vacation properties.

Another factor has been the slow growth of real personal income. Traditional first-home buyers – those in their 20s and 30s – are having difficulty buying a first home, never mind a summer cottage or ski chalet. And the blight on real income growth has also hit older families, slowing their push to a second home.

All these factors combine to make the outlook for second-home price appreciation far less optimistic than it was a decade ago, although the lifetime exemption on capital gains has improved the attractiveness of a second home as an investment.

Commercial property

As a pure investment, commercial property is far more interesting than a second home. Commercial income-producing property includes stores, office buildings, warehouses and residential rentals. Residential rental properties in provinces such as Ontario, where rent controls are in effect, are generally avoided by investors these days.

However, consider the advantages of commercial property. All expenses, including mortgage interest, real estate taxes, and capital cost allowances are deductible for tax purposes from gross income. With the lifetime tax-free capital gains exemption, a portion of capital gains is tax free to the investor.

If your major business is real estate management, losses incurred in conducting a commercial property business are deductible from other income in determining personal taxes. However, you should get advice from a tax professional before assuming you can integrate losses from real estate investment into other personal income. A retired person is likely to qualify, as might a spouse who has a source of personal income, such as that from a trust, and whose only work outside the home is managing the properties.

The value of commercial property

One long-standing rule for determining the value of commercial property dictates that the price should not be more than 10 times net income before financing charges and income taxes. Net income is gross income less all cash expenses, including maintenance and property taxes but excluding mortgage payments.

For example, an older, small store property with a doctor's office upstairs might generate income of $1,000 a month, or $12,000 a year. Maintenance and other cash expenses, including real estate taxes, could be $9,000 annually. So a first approximation of the value of the property is $30,000 – 10 times the $3,000 difference between gross income and cash expenses.

At that price, the investment profile of the property for the first year is as follows:

Cash flow vs. income flow

The $860 pre-tax loss in Table XIX on the next page doesn't mean that the investor is out of pocket by this amount. It simply means that for tax purposes, no income tax is due because income is negative.

In terms of out-of-pocket or cash costs, the building has generated a positive cash inflow of $640. The capital cost allowances are simply a bookkeeping charge against income and do not reflect a cash outlay.

Investment analysis

The analysis of commercial property is identical to that for home ownership. Legal and closing fees, as well as any renovation costs necessary, must be added to the owner's investment. Let's assume in our store-property example that these total $2,000, to which must be added the down payment of $7,500, for combined initial costs of $9,500.

The present value of the annual cash flows must be determined using the investor's required rate of return. Mortgage interest will decline gradually as amortization takes up an increasing portion of the monthly mortgage payment, a factor that will increase cash flow over time. However, other costs, such as real estate taxes and maintenance, may rise. If these offset each other, the building generates a monthly cash flow

---

Table XIX

Property Investment Profile

Gross income	$12,000
Non-financial cash expenses	$9,000
Capital cost allowance*	$1,500
Mortgage interest**	$2,629
Net before income taxes	-$860

*The capital cost allowance is 5% of the unamortized value of the building. So a $30,000 building has a capital cost allowance of $1,500. In the second year, capital costs would drop to 5% of the unamortized value, which is $30,000 less the first year's capital cost allowance ($30,000 minus $1,500). Capital cost allowance in Year 2 amounts to 5% of $28,500, or $1,425. The capital cost allowance in Year 3 would be $1,353.75, or 5% of $27,075 – $30,000 less $1,500, less $1,425. Note that we have assumed that the building is on land that is on long-term lease and is not owned by the investor. Capital cost allowances are not permitted on land, so if the land were part of the investment, its cost would have to be deducted from the cost of the investment to find the depreciable asset investment base on which the 5% would be charged.

**The mortgage assumed is $22,500 at 12% amortized over 25 years for a monthly payment of $232.18, or $2,786.16 a year. However, that includes mortgage amortization, which is not a deductible expense. At the end of the first year the balance outstanding on the mortgage would be $22,342.50, so amortization totaled $157.50 in the first year, bringing mortgage interest in that year to $2,629.

---

of $640 a year with no income-tax liability on building income over a five-year period. On a monthly basis, the cash flow is $53.33.

At an 8% after-tax interest rate, the present value of five years of monthly payments of $1 is $49.32 (see Table XVII). Thus, the present value of $53.33 a month is $2,630.24 ($49.32 times 53.33).

In the home example, remember that the cash flows were all negative. The present value of these negative flows had to be added to the initial cash outlay for the home to find the overall cost. The combination had to be equaled or exceeded by the present value of the market price of the house five years down the road.

In the case of the store property, the cash flows are positive and the present value of the flows should be subtracted from the initial outlay to find the present value of the necessary appreciation of the building in five years. The result is $6,869.76 ($9,500 minus $2,630.24). To find the value of the owner's equity in five years, take the factor $0.681, which is in Table XVI, as the present value of $1 at 8%, and divide it into $6,869.76. You then arrive at a value in five years of $10,087.75.

To find the total required market value of the property in five years, the unamortized portion of the mortgage has to be added to the required increase in equity. From Table XV, we find that a 25-year mortgage at 12% will have $955 outstanding after five years for each $1,000 initially borrowed. So, the outstanding mortgage in five years will be $21,487.50 ($955 times 22.5).

Added to the required value of the equity, the total value of the building in five years must be $31,575.25, an increase of only 5.25% over the entire period, or about 1.03% appreciation annually. The investment should be undertaken if, in your judgment, that rate of price appreciation is equal to or less than what you expect.

Negative cash flows

What if, instead of a positive cash flow, there had been a negative cash flow of $860 a month. The present value of $42,415.20 would then have been added to the $9,500 cost for a total of $51,915.20, which is the present value of the break-even level of equity needed to make the investment acceptable. Dividing by the same 0.681 factor used in Table XVI, the equity value in five years would have to be $76,233.77 ($51,915.20 divided by 0.681).

Add $21,487.50, which represents the unamortized part of the mortgage in five years, and the total value in five years amounts to $97,721.27 ($21,487.50 plus $76,233.77). That means that the value of the property has to grow by more than 325% in five years. In compound interest terms, the property has to manage an annual rate of appreciation of 26.6%.

Unless there are special circumstances that might generate such extraordinary results, such as the opening of a subway station nearby or some other major traffic builder, a reasonable investor would be justified in rejecting this investment.

When the present values of cash flows for a property exceed the initial investment, no further analysis is needed. Just ask the real estate agent where you sign the offer form. Otherwise, the detailed analysis shown above is required.

Negative cash flows do not necessarily mean the investment is bad. They do mean that the value of the property must increase over the investor's planning horizon, and the larger the negative numbers, the larger the price increase that is required. Alternatively, the cash flow from the property should increase in subsequent years as a result of higher rents, decreased expenses or both.

However, negative cash flows, even when justified by future price increases, pose a problem for an investor. They are the equivalent of required monthly payments in a residential home, so the investor must be sure he can afford the monthly payments necessary to cover negative cash flows, regardless of how good the economics look.

Buying a home

If, after examining the rent-or-buy question carefully and after considering your personal preferences, you decide that you do want to buy, the next questions are when and how. Do you buy a home now or wait and risk the possibility that inflation – even at a moderate rate – will push the value up at a faster pace than savings?

There are no easy answers. Housing prices fluctuate like the prices of other goods and services. And while the general trend of housing prices is upward, they have fallen in some areas. The factors to consider before making the plunge include your career path, whether you will remain a two-income household, and your desire to have children. All three have a bearing on whether a family can afford to carry a home without having to submit to a serious change in lifestyle. A person whose income is likely to grow by leaps and bounds in future years can probably risk assuming a large mortgage to buy a home. A spouse's income should be considered in the calculation, but that might eventually be affected by plans for children. You should consider whether you could carry the home on one income. If you can't, are you better off considering a less expensive home?

There are various ways of financing the purchase of a home. But it usually makes sense to make as large a down payment as possible. That's because a large down payment results in smaller mortgage payments and in some cases allows a repayment schedule that increases your equity at a more rapid pace.

Some people buy their homes with moderate down payments, choosing to keep much of their savings in bank and trust company deposits and in certificates and stocks. This makes little sense because mortgage rates exceed deposit rates. And because interest is taxed as income, the after-tax return from fixed-income investments is dwarfed by the mortgage rate.

Mortgage interest is generally not deductible as an expense for tax purposes. So you should consider paying off your mortgage as a risk-free investment. In fact, you probably couldn't get an after-tax rate of return exceeding your mortgage rate from any investment.

If you have investments and a mortgage and feel you want both, consider the following strategy: Sell your investments and pay off your mortgage, then borrow against the equity in your home and buy a similar portfolio back. You'll still own a comparable portfolio and owe the same amount of money as before. But now your loan is for investment purposes, so the interest is deductible from income for tax purposes.

What lenders look for

Lenders look at two figures when considering a mortgage: your down payment relative to the value of the home and your income.

Institutions generally won't lend more than 75% of a property's value unless the amount above 75% is covered by mortgage insurance. With mortgage insurance, an institution will lend up to 90% of the property's value. High-ratio mortgages, as they are called, are expensive, usually costing a couple of percentage points more than conventional mortgages. An alternative to a high-ratio mortgage is a second mortgage, which makes sense if you are buying a home and assuming an existing mortgage with favorable terms. While second mortgages are available from mortgage brokers, your bank or trust company is the first place you should try.

Many lenders have also put a ceiling on the values of properties against which they will lend 75%, especially in markets where house prices have skyrocketed in recent years. Lenders are concerned that if housing prices fall they might find the values of some properties falling below the values of their loans.

Shop for a mortgage

Lately, the mortgage market has been a strong area for lenders. As a result, financial institutions are competitive and will usually come up with terms to suit your needs. For instance, some will rewrite an existing mortgage when a house is sold, raising the loan amount and adjusting the payment to reflect a blend of current interest rates and the rate in effect when the mortgage was originally arranged.

New homes generally have financing in place when you buy. But if the home is a resale, the vendor will often take back a mortgage. However, you would probably be better off arranging your own financing before making an offer for a home if the existing financing is inadequate. By arranging your own funds, you can make an unconditional offer and possibly get the house at a lower price.

It's best to shop for financing before you make an offer on a house. See your bank, trust company or credit union manager to discuss your intentions and determine the size of the loan for which you will qualify. The rule of thumb followed by some institutions is that mortgage payments, property taxes and heating expenses should not exceed 32% of your gross income. Those amounts, plus other consumer debt such as car payments, should not exceed 37% of income.

Your choice of term

Your mortgage will probably be amortized over 25 years. But the term over which interest rates are fixed will be less – one to five years in most cases. People who feel rates will remain low or move lower usually go for short terms, while people who are nervous about the direction of rates usually go for longer terms.

Your choice of term should reflect not only your views on the direction of rates but your ability to take risk. Sometimes you might be better off locking in a rate for a longer term if only to have the peace of mind that your mortgage payments won't change for several years – no matter what happens to interest rates. If your mortgage comes up for renewal in a period of high rates and you think they might tumble, see if the mortgage holder will give you an open mortgage or a floating-rate mortgage. With these you'll be able to renegotiate your mortgage to a longer-term fixed rate if rates subsequently fall.

If you need a mortgage or have one coming up for renewal, it pays to shop well in advance to find the best deals. It might not pay to move from one lender to another, especially since you are likely to incur legal fees and pay for an appraisal of your home. However, some institutions will pay a portion of the costs involved in moving a mortgage from another lender. If you find a rate lower than the one your lender has offered, see if your lender will match the competing bid.

Before buying a home, inspect it thoroughly so you're aware of any faults or potential repairs. Many people use inspection services, which for a few hundred dollars look over the house, reporting on the condition of its electrical system, plumbing, heating system and other features.

Selling a home, like selling any other investment, also incurs costs. But a house is one of the few investments you can sell on your own. However, it is a difficult, time-consuming task. So most people who decide to sell turn to a real estate broker. With dozens of firms to choose from in most cities, finding the one that's best for you can be wearisome.

The quest for competence

Finding a competent real estate broker and agent is extremely important. A poor choice could mean your home will sit on the market for months because it was listed at an unrealistically high price. Conversely, you don't want your home sold at a price substantially below its value.

When properly chosen, a broker will get you the best possible price quickly. The agent will screen out sightseers and show the house to more potential buyers than a homeowner can. And a good broker can come up with financing to help potential buyers make a deal.

The cost of a broker is not cheap. Commissions range from 4% to 6% of the selling price for an exclusive listing, with the rate dependent on the value of the home and market conditions. Including the home under a multiple listing service costs another percentage point, but it exposes your home to many brokers and their clients. And don't expect to negotiate the commission rate, even though technically it is negotiable. In reality, rates in most markets are fixed (although this is changing because of government pressure.)

Choosing a broker

When the time comes to choose a broker, talk with three or four before making a decision. Ask each to come to your home to appraise its value and discuss how he proposes to sell it. The brokers you invite should have plenty of experience in your neighborhood. It doesn't matter whether the firms are national, independent, franchise operations or trust company agents. It does matter that they are successful at selling homes in your area.

If you're not familiar with a firm's roster of agents, call the owner or manager and insist that the agent sent to deal with you is experienced and has sold extensively in your neighborhood. It is also important that the agent be experienced in selling your type of home – it makes little sense to have someone who specializes in moderately priced homes if yours is a rambling mansion.

Agents should be prepared to suggest a selling price, backed by recent sales figures of homes in your area. You should be made aware of listing prices, selling prices and how long the homes were on the market. You should also be shown listings of homes that didn't sell because of high prices.

An agent who does not arrive properly prepared, or who cannot back up an evaluation with data, should be rejected. Similarly, reject any agent who does not ask about existing mortgages and who has no suggestions about financing. Financing arrangements can often make or break a sale.

Most homes have mortgages held by banks, trust companies or insurance companies. A good agent will first determine whether the holder will be willing to rewrite the mortgage for the purchaser. Many financial institutions will do this routinely, so be wary of any agent who suggests a financing alternative before checking to see what can be done with the existing mortgage.

The agent should also present a strategy for selling your home. Most will ask for an exclusive listing, which may be for 90 days. In return for this, the broker will spend some money advertising your home. Determine the firm's advertising policy and look at recent issues of the daily newspaper to determine if homes listed with the firm get good exposure. On any given day a firm may advertise only a few of the homes it has listed in a neighborhood, but its agents would probably show several homes to anyone responding to an advertisement.

Once you make your choice, the agent will give you a listing agreement to sign. It is a binding contract appointing the firm as your agent for a limited time, so your lawyer should examine the agreement before you sign it. Many listing agreements state that a commission is payable for procuring an acceptable offer. In other words, the broker gets paid even if the deal doesn't close. Many lawyers insist that this clause be changed so the commissions are paid only if the actual sale takes place. If the deal doesn't close, the vendor should be entitled to keep the deposit made by the potential buyer. This compensates for lost time and legal expenses.

Do-it-yourself sale

Many people are capable of selling their own homes, but this can be a time-consuming task and individuals often make errors in assessing the values of their homes. However, the saving on commission is reason enough to consider acting as your own broker. Remember, however, that in private sales the buyer often thinks he should get the benefit of commission savings.

If you decide to bypass a broker, set a realistic price. This can be determined by checking recent sales in your neighborhood. It makes sense to hire an independent appraiser, who for a fee of $200 to $300 will give you a written report on the value of your home. The appraisal itself can be an excellent sales tool. Check with the mortgage departments of several banks, trust companies and insurance companies for names of appraisers they use. Most institutions will accept an appraisal as proof of value for mortgage financing. You can then take the appraisal to the institution that holds the mortgage on your property to determine the amount it would lend to a purchaser who meets its requirements.

You should also advertise your home. A simple sign on your lawn is essential, but make sure it says "by appointment only" so you can control who comes in and when. Your newspaper advertisements – budget at least $500 for a long-term campaign – should list the location of your home, type of home, the number of rooms and outstanding features.

The price you quote should be about 5% higher than the price you expect to get in order to leave room for haggling. Make sure your lawyer knows what you're doing and show him every offer you are considering. Remember, once your signature appears on the offer, it becomes a binding contract. In addition, let your lawyer know about any outstanding liens against your property so arrangements can be made to deal with them before your home is sold. An offer should be accompanied by a substantial deposit – 10% of the selling price, according to some experts. It will be held by your lawyer in trust until the sale closes.

CHAPTER TWELVE

OPTIONS: HEAVEN OR HELL IN THE MARKET

SO YOU'RE LOOKING FOR AN INVESTMENT THAT WILL DOUBLE YOUR money overnight – or at least within a week.

It's rare for stocks to perform that well. But the doubling of investors' money is fairly common in the options markets. Options can be a speculator's paradise, or they can be a place to quickly lose your shirt in a few days. Ironically, options are also used by conservative investors as a vehicle to reduce risk. Indeed some analysts blame the volatility of stock markets – particularly the sharp price declines of October 1987 – on institutional use of options and futures contracts to hedge exposure through computer "program trading." (More on this later.)

Options are the right to buy or sell a specific security, currency or commodity at a given price until a set date. There are options on stocks, bonds, currencies, stock market indexes, gold, silver and bonds. Much of the growth in options trading in Canada is a relatively recent development. They were first introduced on the Toronto Stock Exchange in 1975 for blue-chip stocks such as Bell Canada. In 1987 the TSE introduced options on a new market index, the Toronto 35, giving institutional investors a new instrument for hedging their portfolios. Even so, the options market is still "thin," which means there isn't a massive amount of trading. However, it has been picking up.

There are two types of options – calls and puts. A call option on a stock gives the holder the right to buy 100 shares of a specific stock (the underlying security) at a fixed price until a given date. A put option gives the right to sell the shares at a specified price by a certain date. For example, an XYZ Ltd. February $17.50 call option gives the holder the right to buy 100 shares of XYZ at $17.50 until the third Friday in February.

Maturity dates for options are standard. There are three maturity cycles: January, April, July and October; February, May, August and November; and March, June, September and December. Each option trades in one cycle only, and the longest option contract is nine months. Exercise prices are standard as well, but there can be several options available on the same stock with the same maturity date and with different exercise prices. This would happen if a stock price were to move sharply. New options would be created using $2.50 intervals for stocks selling below $50.

Option contracts are issued by a clearing corporation – such as Trans Canada Options Inc., which is responsible for guaranteeing that all parties involved meet their obligations. You can trade options through any stockbroker registered to deal in options.

The option itself is liquid and marketable. Its value is called the premium, which consists of the difference between the stock price and the exercise price, plus the value the market places on the time remaining before the option expires. Using our XYZ example, if the stock trades at $19 and the $17.50 call option trades at $3, the option price, or premium, is made up of $1.50 in difference between the price of the stock and the exercise price plus $1.50 in time value placed on the option by the market. The time value can quickly disappear as the option approaches maturity.

If you buy an option at $3 and the stock price moves almost immediately to $22, you would expect the option to appreciate by about $3 as well, so you would double your money. Compare your potential return against what you would have gained by buying the stock. However, if you bought the stock and it failed to move, you would dispose of the option prior to the exercise date at $1.50 – the difference between the stock price and the exercise price. This means you would lose half your money, plus whatever commissions you must pay.

Playing the options market can be risky, and many people quickly lose all their capital. But the potential rewards are great, and that's what entices investors. A good rule of thumb is to not use more than 10% to 20% of your total investment capital when buying options. And if you're going to speculate in options on stocks, stick to options on securities that have historically been more volatile than the general market. For example, if you buy call options because you think the market is going higher, go for options on stocks that tend to do better than the market when it is rising. Conversely, if you are buying put options, go for options on underlying securities that tend to tumble when the general market moves lower.

Some people participate in the options market in a more conservative way. They "write" options to reduce the risk of losing money on their portfolios. In other words, they sell options against stocks they own.

For example, ABC Ltd. may trade at $20. An investor buying at this price might decide to sell an August $22 call option contract against the holding at $2. This investor has now reduced his cost by $2, which acts a cushion if the stock declines. If the stock moves up, but doesn't exceed $22, the investor won't see the option exercised, so he will not only have the premium but will keep the stock. If the stock moves above $22 at the exercise date, the option will be exercised and the investor's broker will turn over the shares to the options exchange or clearing corporation at $22, making the investor a profit of $4 before commissions.

You can, of course, purchase an option to cover your liability. For instance, if the stock price fell to $18, the premium would fall too. An investor might purchase the option back at a fraction of its previous sale price and then sell another option on it, exercisable at a lower price.

You shouldn't be too concerned if a call option is exercised against you. The price of the premium is usually great enough that the likelihood of your shares being called is slim. And if the shares are called, you will earn a significant return on your capital.

You can also sell options without owning the underlying security. However, this is extremely risky because your exposure is unlimited, while your maximum profit is the premium you've received. For example, you might sell an option that can be exercised at $20, only to find that a takeover offer is suddenly made at $60 a share. Your option could be called, forcing you to buy shares at $60 to satisfy your obligation. Few brokers recommend writing "naked calls" because it's a dangerous strategy for the client and the broker if something goes sour.

Options trading has become much more sophisticated in recent years with the development of computer programs that calculate potential profits using assumptions about where the markets might move. Options departments at most major brokerage firms have these programs in use for their retail and institutional clients.

Program trading is an extension of these facilities. With program trading, a large financial institution attempts to hedge against swings in the value of its portfolio by using futures contracts and general index options. For instance, a portfolio manager might sell an index option or futures contract against the value of the portfolio to lock in profits. If the index fell, the gain in the price of the futures or the premium from the option would offset any decline in the value of the portfolio.

In thin markets, the values of options and futures get out of line with the values of underlying securities. Picture a system where computers monitor portfolio, options and futures prices and trigger trades to take advantage of price differences (known as arbitrage). Now imagine what happens when a computer triggers trades in a thin, volatile market. Buying and selling pressures send prices even more out of line, thus increasing the volatility of the market. In the U.S., where some people in the investment business see program trading as a problem, measures have been taken to reduce the volatility by restricting the magnitude of price movements.

Individual investors can use options to stabilize their returns or as an alternative to holding stocks. For example, if you have realized substantial paper profits and are worried about the market moving lower, you might take your profits and use some of your gain to buy call options to participate in further gains available in the near term. Alternatively, you might sell call options against your portfolio, giving you a cushion if prices decline.

You can play the same game with put options. Rather than selling your shares, paying a commission, and possibly using up some of your lifetime capital gains exemption, you could continue to hold the stock and buy put options. If your shares continue to rise, your profits will grow and the put options you bought will be worthless when they expire. But if the stocks reverse, your put options will appreciate in value, offsetting any declines. When you use call and put options to lock in profits, consider your costs as insurance.

You can also sell put options. But by doing this you commit yourself to buy a specific stock at a specific price, even if it is well below the market price. Selling put options is a strategy you might use if you want to buy a specific stock but feel it is too expensive. By selling a put option you can potentially get the stock at a lower price if it pulls back. And if it doesn't, you're still ahead of the game because you've received a premium for your efforts.

Buying put options is an alternative to "short selling," which involves borrowing shares from your broker, then selling them with the intention of buying them back at a later date at a lower price. In this case, the difference in price at which you borrow and the price at which you buy represents your profit. Selling short incurs unlimited liability, while buying puts limits your risk to the cost of the put.

Similarly, you can use index options to protect your entire portfolio. The TSE 35 Index was created specifically to allow the trading of options and futures based on a basket of liquid, widely held stocks found in many institutional portfolios.

Options can also be used for some fairly conservative strategies. You could, for instance put 95% of your money in treasury bills and 5% in call or put options. If properly used, this strategy will protect your capital while giving you an opportunity to participate in market movements. And you don't have to tie this type of strategy to stock options; you can also use bond options if your objective is to profit from moves in interest rates.

There are numerous strategies that employ more than one option in order to limit potential losses in options trading. The thing to remember is that any strategy that limits losses usually puts a ceiling on profits. For example, you might write one call and one put against the same security. You would earn two premiums, thereby reducing your cost and earning a profit if the price increases. You could lose, however, if the stock fell sharply and you were "put," meaning you would have to buy more shares as the puts were exercised.

Options strategies are quite complex and many investors make the mistake of ignoring commissions when they calculate their potential returns. Commissions can be significant and should be included in any calculation, although they will vary, depending on what type of dealer you chose. You can do business with a full-service dealer or a discounter with low commissions. If you need advice, information and the use of a dealer's option expertise, the full-service dealer will prove good value. Just make sure the broker you choose has extensive experience in options and the firm has the latest technical equipment to give you the information you need to make the best decision.

You should also familiarize yourself with the language of options and learn some of the terms involved. Most dealers can provide you with literature on options, and some offer seminars on the topic.

You'll encounter phrases such as "in-the-money options," "intrinsic value," "opening-purchase transaction," "opening-sale transaction" and "straddles." Here are some explanations of terms used in options trading:

In-the-money Option: In the case of a call option, this is an option for which the stock price is higher than the exercise price. In the case of a put option, the stock price is lower.

Out-of-the-money Option: In the case of a call option, this is an option for which the stock price is lower than the exercise price. For a put option, the stock price is higher than the exercise price.

Intrinsic Value: The difference between the stock and exercise prices when an option is in the money.

Opening-purchase Transaction: A transaction in which an investor buys an option.

Opening-sale Transaction: A transaction in which an investor writes an option. The writer is the seller of an option contract.

Straddle: A strategy that involves buying or selling both puts and calls. A straddle is an order to buy or sell the same number of put and call options on the same underlying stock for the same exercise price and expiration date.

Time Spread: Also known as calendar spread and horizontal spread, this refers to the practice of holding options with the same exercise price but with different expiration dates.

Price Spread: This involves the holding of options with different exercise prices but with the same expiration date.

Diagonal Spread: A combination of time spread and price spread.

CHAPTER THIRTEEN

COMMODITIES, CURRENCIES AND FUTURES

STORIES ABOUND OF PEOPLE STARTING OFF WITH NEXT TO NOTHING and becoming millionaires in a matter of days by playing the futures markets.

There are also plenty of stories about people losing everything in the futures market. They're true, too. They just aren't as popular as the tales of success.

Depending on who you listen to, the futures markets are either one of the few places huge amounts of capital can be quickly accumulated or they're a path to financial disaster where you can lose your shirt in minutes. In fact, both can happen. But many novices jump into commodities without fully considering how risky they can be. When things go wrong, you can lose not only your investment money, but just about everything you own. If you want to dabble in the futures markets, it is imperative that you understand what futures are and the purpose of the markets.

Special delivery

A futures contract is an obligation that covers the delivery of a specific amount of a commodity, currency or security at a specified future date at a specific price. The amounts are standard, such as 112,000 pounds of sugar, 100 ounces of gold or 12.5 million Japanese yen.

You can also invest in stock index futures that involve a cash settlement, rather than delivery of a stock portfolio. For example, one type of futures contract is based on the Toronto Stock Exchange's index of 35 stocks. You aren't required to deliver a basket of 35 stocks, but you must settle with an amount of cash based on the index's closing value on the third Friday of the month.

Even if you buy commodity futures, you needn't worry about having 112,000 pounds of sugar dumped on your lawn – unless you really want delivery. Instead, your broker would automatically buy or sell an offsetting contract prior to the delivery date.

The original hedge

Futures markets were established to allow commodity producers – farmers, mining companies and lumber companies among them – and commodity purchasers such as food processing companies, metal fabricators and lumber dealers, to hedge against price swings. The major North American commodity exchanges are in Chicago and New York, and they deal with a variety of commodities, including grains, meats, cotton, lumber, coffee, sugar, livestock and metals such as gold and silver. In addition, exchanges trade in currencies and interest-rate futures as well as stock market futures. In Canada, the Toronto Futures Exchange and the Montreal Exchange specialize in contracts tied to securities and precious metals.

The large players in the markets are hedgers. For example, a farmer who is worried that the price of wheat might be lower at harvest time might decide to sell some of his anticipated production in the futures market. But he will not necessarily deliver wheat on the contract date; instead he is likely to buy another contract to cancel the one he sold. If his prediction of lower prices is correct, he will buy a contract at a price lower than that for which he sold a contract. The difference (his profit) will help offset the low prices received for his crop.

However, if he's wrong and prices move higher at harvest time, he'll take a loss in the futures market. But he'll still get more for his crop, so in the long term hedging allows him to stabilize his income. Similarly, users of commodities may want to lock in a price months or even a year in advance of taking delivery by buying futures contracts to hedge against wide price swings.

Something for everyone

Who uses futures markets to hedge? Everyone from major gold producers to the operators of small businesses who want protection against changing currency values. For instance, a Canadian retailer who buys merchandise in New York may worry that the Canadian dollar will tumble before the goods are delivered. He could lock in an exchange rate using the futures market. Importers can also deal with their banks in what is known as the forward market, whereby a bank will specify an exchange rate for a specific amount and a specific date.

But to be efficient, the market requires a large number of participants. There aren't enough farmers and food processors to give the market liquidity, but there are enough speculators. They trade in futures not because they want to hedge, but because they are trying to make a financial killing.

A matter of leverage

Futures markets are risky because of the leverage involved. Unlike stock markets, where investors have to put up at least half the value of a stock when they make a purchase, futures markets require only a small portion of the total value of a contract. It is possible to buy a contract valued at about US$100,000 (most contracts are quoted in U.S. funds, including some traded in Canada) with only $2,000 tied up as margin or good faith money.

If the value of a $100,000 futures contract tumbles by, for instance, 5% in a given day, a trader who is "long," or obligated to buy, would have to come up with an additional $5,000 to maintain his margin position. If the trader doesn't have the necessary funds, the position will be sold out by the broker and the trader will lose his initial investment and be responsible for the difference.

How do people make millions? By pyramiding their positions. If that same commodity goes up 5%, a trader would then buy additional contracts with his new equity and continue to add more as the price rises. But if the trend reverses, watch out. Equity will quickly evaporate, leaving the trader responsible for additional losses.

The risks inherent in commodities futures markets is underlined by the fact that a broker will allow you to open a trading account only after you've read and signed some detailed forms that spell out the risks. But that doesn't mean everybody reads the forms carefully before signing. Many investors begin to understand the risks only when they face substantial losses.

Beginner's luck

The biggest pitfall facing beginners in the futures market is lack of experience. Although individuals with beginner's luck may make money in the beginning, they don't always hang on to it. At the end of 1979 it was possible to buy a gold contract for about US$500 an ounce. A few weeks later, gold peaked at $850. As prices rose, some investors used their growing equity to finance additional purchases. When the trend reversed, they lost heavily.

Even the experts get burned. Take the rapid price decline of silver, which tumbled in early 1980 from US$50 an ounce to about $12. Brokers and players, including the legendary Hunt brothers of Texas, lost hundreds of millions of dollars.

Both silver and gold fell sharply – gold to below $300 an ounce in early 1985 and silver to less than $6. However, fortunes were made by those who were able to ride the downtrend.

Many beginners think they can protect themselves by issuing stop-loss orders. These are orders to liquidate positions if the price reaches a certain level, with the aim of limiting losses. While stop-loss orders are something speculators should consider, they must also realize that such orders don't always limit risk. A commodity price can decline for a number of days without any futures trading taking place. When the stop-loss is finally executed, the loss may greatly exceed the amount originally projected.

Because of the potential volatility of commodities markets – for example, the sharp rise in orange juice futures on news of a heavy, unexpected frost – mechanisms have been put in place to restrict price movements, including limits on how far a price is allowed to move up or down in a day.

Who should play?

If you intend to play the futures markets, make sure you understand the risks, that you can live with them and, most important, that you can afford them. There are no hard and fast rules about who should or should not get involved with commodities or other futures. But anyone interested should first realize that for every winner there is a loser, and in some cases the person on the other side of the trade is a lot more knowledgeable about the factors affecting the price of a specific commodity. If you want to trade in coffee or sugar, for example, odds are that the trader for a food processing company who may be on the other side of the trade will almost certainly know more about the relevant markets than you do.

Then there's the matter of cost. Most brokers want only clients who can afford the risks. Some won't take clients who have a net worth of less than $250,000, excluding their homes and cars. These people should probably restrict the futures portion of their holdings to 10%, and they should be prepared to lose that 10%. Many experienced futures brokers will also refuse to accept as clients people who seem unable to handle the stress that trading commodities futures produces. And if you have a history of losing money in the stock market, stay out of futures; you'd probably end up losing even more – possibly everything you own.

Many beginners make the same errors, which explains why most investors lose money on commodities. Using the pyramiding strategy unsuccessfully is one of those errors. There is a tendency among traders and brokers to pyramid positions, which, as the gold example shows, increases the trader's risk. A minor setback puts the trader in a major loss position. Another common error is holding too large a position in one account. The markets are simply too volatile for investors to put all their eggs in one basket.

The key decision

If you decide to invest in commodities, your key decision will be your choice of broker. With a good broker you might make money – possibly a great deal of money. More important, a good broker won't let you get into a position where you could lose everything.

Most brokerage houses will check your credit rating. Don't withhold information about other commodity accounts because you are embarrassed about your previous losses. The industry is small enough that your omission will be discovered. And remember, you make the decisions, not your broker. His or her job is to advise and guide you, and keep you out of trouble. But you're the one who places the order and accepts the consequences.

Of course, you should check your broker out thoroughly. Deal only with an established firm. Most are affiliated with major stock brokerage houses or are members of futures exchanges, including the Toronto Futures Exchange.

The research provided by brokers to their clients is fairly standard and consists of industry studies, technical analysis of trends and news reports of developments that affect prices. Some firms have computerized trading models that can be used to provide trading discipline with the objective of cutting losses and letting profits ride.

Some people may want to consider buying units, or shares, of one of the commodity funds offered from time to time by major brokerage houses. They offer the advantages of professional management, diversification and limited risk. With these funds you can't lose more you than put in.

Ask yourself, "How much can I lose?" – not "How much can I make?" Of course, you can lower your risk by putting up more margin in the form of U.S. government treasury bills. But most people who play the commodities futures market are interested in speculating rather than limiting risk.

As with options, there are numerous trading strategies you can follow to limit your risk. Most futures dealers can provide detailed information on how such trading strategies can be used to your advantage.

CHAPTER FOURTEEN

GOLD AND SILVER: MONEY THAT IS REAL

IT'S DIFFICULT FOR SOME PEOPLE TO UNDERSTAND WHY GOLD, SILVER and other precious metals are considered investments. After all, gold doesn't pay dividends or interest.

Conversely, there are many people who can't understand why anyone would sink all his money into securities issued or guaranteed by governments, given the history of paper money around the world. Indeed, inflation has eroded the value of paper money in most countries over the years.

The facts are that precious metals have proven to be a store of value through periods of inflation, political upheaval, war and social unrest. In addition, gold is a historical and universal medium of exchange. But putting everything you own into precious metals can be risky if the prices that people are willing to pay for them gets out of whack with reality.

Take the events of late 1979 and early 1980. People were lining up at banks, coin dealers and precious metals dealers to buy gold and silver. Inflation was higher than interest rates, so people who put their money in banks to earn interest were net losers, even before taxes. As a result, people flocked to buy tangibles. In just a decade, gold moved from about US$40 an ounce to its early-1980 high of $850. Silver followed a similar pattern, peaking at US$50 an ounce. (Gold and silver prices are quoted worldwide in U.S. dollars in both troy ounces and metric weights.)

Then the bubble burst and prices plunged. In mid-1988, gold was trading at about $450 an ounce, up more than 50% from its post-1980 lows. Silver was trading at around $7. Undoubtedly, fortunes have been made by traders who have caught the many swings in precious metals since the early 1970s, when the U.S. government decided to stop selling gold at $35 an ounce and redeeming its silver-certificate one-dollar bills for silver dollars. But fortunes have been lost by people who misunderstood the markets and allowed greed to rule their decisions.

If you put everything you own into gold and silver, you become a gambler, betting that currencies and securities that pay interest are going to lose much of their value – like the German mark did in the 1920s. However, if you put 5% to 15% of your assets in precious metals, you can classify yourself as a hedger, holding precious metals as a hedge against a sharp increase in inflation or political turbulence.

Gold, silver and other tangible investments, such as diamonds, rise in inflationary periods when people are worried that the purchasing power of their money is being eroded. They rise most when the spread between nominal interest rates and inflation is shrinking or when inflation exceeds nominal interest rates. They do poorly when people can do better by putting their money in interest-bearing securities.

Sometimes politics helps gold and silver. Worries about political unrest in different parts of the world send money looking for havens. Sometimes the haven is the U.S. dollar; other times it's gold.

Inflation hasn't been a big problem lately, so gold and silver have been in the doldrums. But many investors continue to hold a portion of their assets in precious metals as a hedge against inflation.

Poor man's gold

Silver is sometimes described as poor man's gold. Its price tends to be more volatile and, because of the metal's widespread industrial use, it may not always move with gold. Silver can also be more susceptible than gold to movement by groups of buyers. That was the case in 1979 and early 1980, when a group tried to corner the silver market and its value increased fivefold before crashing.

There are several ways to buy gold. You can buy the metal itself in the form of wafers and bars, or in coins such as the Canadian Maple Leaf. You can also buy gold certificates, which are backed by the assets of the issuer but not necessarily by gold itself. You can buy shares of gold mining companies and you can even invest in gold through mutual funds that hold the metals themselves, shares in precious metals companies or both.

Gold shares tend to outperform gold bullion when prices are rising. But bullion tends to fall less than gold shares when bullion prices decline. Many people prefer bullion because it is a tangible investment.

Bullion is sold in bars and wafers in a wide range of weights from five grams to standard bars of 400 ounces. The gold prices quoted in newspapers generally apply to 400-ounce purchases and sales.

Bullion has a number of advantages for the investor. It is easily marketable worldwide. It is probably the least expensive way of buying gold because commissions and other charges are small. And it can be purchased in some provinces without paying sales tax. The disadvantages of holding gold bullion include storage and insurance fees, and possible assay charges if you sell after the gold has been in your possession.

Banks and dealers that sell gold to the public quote prices based on 400-ounce bars. On a given day they may bid for gold at, say, $464 an ounce and sell it at $467.

But few people have the resources to buy 400-ounce bars. Instead, they purchase smaller amounts and pay a bit more per ounce to cover manufacturing charges. These bar charges range from about $1.10 an ounce for a 100-ounce bar to $3.35 for a one-ounce wafer to $15 an ounce for a five-gram wafer (0.161 ounces). You do not pay a premium when you sell.

The prices quoted for silver by dealers are for 1,000-ounce bars, but you can buy smaller sizes, ranging from one ounce to 100 ounces. A one-kilogram bar, which contains 32.150 fine ounces of silver, is also available. The premium for a one-ounce wafer is about $3, which makes a small purchase proportionately expensive.

You have to consider other possible charges. There may be delivery fees, and even a small commission. One bank recently quoted a commission of 0.25% on transactions of less than US$5,000 and 0.125% on transactions in excess of $5,000. Storage charges are about 0.375% on the first $50,000 of gold bullion held and 0.125% on the balance (of market value). For silver, charges are fractionally higher.

Bullion is available from some banks, some trust companies, bullion dealers and a handful of stock brokerage houses. You should choose your dealer with care, and the novice is best off dealing with a bank or trust company. Remember, however, that they are dealers and it isn't their responsibility to dispense advice on price trends.

Certificates and coins

If you don't want to take delivery of your gold, certificates are available. They can be converted into bullion, with delivery usually taking place within 30 days. They are also negotiable outside of Canada at certain institutions. However, they aren't always backed by gold; instead, they are backed by the general assets of the institution from which the certificates are purchased. That's why you should buy certificates only from stable institutions.

Certificates are usually sold in minimum amounts of 10 ounces of gold and 50 ounces of silver. Storage and administration charges are minor – only a few cents a day per 100 ounces. However, you could face manufacturing charges if you trade your certificate for the real thing.

One advantage of certificates is that you can buy them in fractional weights, calculated to three decimal places. This means that you can purchase $1,000 of gold, which at the time of writing would entitle you to a certificate for 2.222 ounces (ignoring premiums and other charges).

Coins and certificates for coins are also popular. The South African krugerrand one-ounce gold coin was until the mid-1980s the favorite of buyers worldwide. But its popularity has waned at the hands of the Canadian Maple Leaf and coins issued by the U.S., Mexico, China and Australia. Few major dealers still sell the krugerrand. But people holding them have no trouble getting full value if they sell (less minor charges). After all, gold is gold, no matter what is stamped on it.

The Maple Leaf is available in one-ounce, half-ounce, quarter-ounce and one-tenth ounce sizes and is readily marketable anywhere. The coins trade at a premium above the price of bullion. For example, you would be able to buy a Maple Leaf coin for about $482 if bullion is trading at $467. That's a premium of about 4%. You could sell a a Maple Leaf for about $476 when bullion is selling at about $464 an ounce, a premium of about 3%. If you live in certain provinces, you will also have to pay sales taxes on gold coins. For example, Ontario and British Columbia charge 8% and Quebec charges 9%. There is no sales tax on coins in Alberta.

You can also buy what are known as numismatic coins. They sell at prices above the value of the bullion they contain, and appeal to collectors. Their price reflects their scarcity as well as their gold content, but they are less marketable than bullion coins.

Playing gold stocks

Gold share prices reflect gold price expectations as well as companies' production, profits, dividend payments and the outlook for new discoveries. The gold stocks market is highly specialized, but it can be divided into three major categories: Tier I companies, which are major producers and generally have large market capitalizations; Tier II companies, which are medium producers of about 200,000 ounces annually; and Tier III companies, which are exploration plays that have yet to produce gold. There are also those companies that have yet to discover gold, but which have promising properties.

The prices of shares in companies that produce and pay dividends tend to be less volatile than those of junior exploration companies. Yet they are still more volatile than the prices of most other stocks, and juniors are most volatile. So if you want to invest in the junior gold stocks, you should first decide whether you can afford the risks. If you can't, stay away.

Much of the recent action in gold has been in North American stocks, particularly as many institutional investors move out of South African holdings. But Canadian investors can still buy shares of South African gold mining companies through any broker. Some investors find them attractive because their dividend yields are higher than those of Canadian gold mining shares.

Gold mutual funds make sense for investors who want a diversified precious metals portfolio. As with other mutual funds, the advantage here is that of professional management.

Precious stones

In the past decade or so, diamonds and other gemstones have grown more appealing to investors, particularly during periods of high inflation. However, their prices can be very volatile and, just like gold and silver, plunged sharply during early 1980. Diamonds are a highly specialized area of investment, and are definitely not for the beginner.

The key points to remember: No two diamonds are alike, even if they are in the same class and are of the same weight; and unlike commodities, gold and stocks, diamonds are not sold in an auction market.

Diamonds differ from gold in that you cannot obtain a price quote over the telephone or buy and sell at the same price throughout the world. To determine a diamond price, you must obtain an appraisal. Moreover, the spreads between the bid price and ask price are substantial. Unlike gold, where the markup is usually less than 1%, the markup on diamonds can be 100% to 200%. In other words, the price has to double for you to break even, unless you can buy at cost. On top of that, unless you're buying smuggled diamonds, you're paying a hefty federal tax and duty.

Diamonds do have their uses as investments, particularly in parts of the world where people are looking for hedges against political upheaval. After all, it's easier to flee a country with $100,000 of diamonds than with $100,000 of gold.

If you want to invest in diamonds, stick to top quality stones of about one carat. Larger ones may prove difficult to sell because the market is thin. And buy only from reputable dealers. More than one person has purchased industrial-grade stones thinking they were jewelry quality. Others have been fooled into buying synthetic stones, believing them to be the real thing. Some experts suggest that investors buy and store their stones outside Canada to avoid paying duties and sales taxes.

Colored stones are an alternative to diamonds. But the market for these gems is more fragmented than the diamond market, and there are no standard grading systems.

CHAPTER FIFTEEN

THE ART OF INVESTING IN ART

SOME PEOPLE ARGUE THAT A SIGNIFICANT PORTION OF YOUR PERSONAL wealth should be in art. After all, substantial art collectors are often wealthy businessmen. Many of the significant public collections put together in modern times, such as the art in the National Galleries in Washington, D.C., and the Getty Museum in California, were made possible by business tycoons such as J.P. Getty.

Maybe so. But you might have second thoughts – not about buying art, but about investing in art – after reading this section.

The hype artists

Art as an investment is pushed by art auction houses and fancy dealers. Without high art prices, art sellers could not afford expensive rented premises and the good things in life. So, although good dealers and auction house people usually know a fair amount about art, they clearly have a vested interest. But art is what counts, not money. So the suave dealer peddling a $10,000 piece of art can become downright contemptuous if you ask what the investment prospects are for his treasure. He may well reply: "If you are interested in money, buy bonds." For some reason, he will seldom refer to the stock market, where the risks more closely reflect the art market. The world of art is in many ways like the world of stocks. Just like there are established artists and new artists, there are established stocks and there are new issues. There are stocks for which there are always buyers, although not always at the best price, and there are stocks for which the market disappears at the first sign of a cloud.

What the art dealer wants to do, as does the auctioneer who wears formal dress to peddle paintings, is to intimidate you. Your $10,000 is as real to the dealer as it is to you. But the major difference is this: until you have bought the painting, the $10,000 is yours, not his. You could like the painting but feel that unless the price of the piece will appreciate by at least the rate paid by your friendly bank, it is beyond your means.

Of course, dealers don't have the slightest notion of how fast the price will rise, or if it will rise at all. So they take the noble posture of being above mere money. Still, the dealer and everyone involved in selling art has to rely on hype that implies fast returns if they are to make sales.

One of the schemes used by art dealers is announcements of record prices. The art auction season, which traditionally runs from late October through late May, but actually extends as long as the major art auction companies think they can attract enough money to make an auction profitable, has become the focus of the announcements.

Dealers often view auction houses as competition, even though their relationship is symbiotic, with auction houses providing at least some degree of liquidity to the art market. If there were no auction houses, it would be even more difficult for collectors to unload their treasures. Dealers would have to provide liquidity themselves or sell less at lower prices. Auction houses also serve as a means through which dealers can efficiently adjust inventories.

Auction houses and dealers both benefit from announcements of record prices, even though the announcements are made by auction houses. The most potent announcement is the establishment of the highest price ever achieved for a painting widely viewed as a masterpiece, or the highest price for a work painted by a particular master. The media report the record price, and dealers and auction houses let their clients know.

The problem with the record announcement approach is that, to get a world record price, you need a very unusual and beautiful piece of art. These, by definition, are rare. So the auction houses often lack items of rarity and beauty.

Trying to create gold from dross

Caught in a booming art market, some greedy dealers and auction houses work rapidly to bringing new artists to the $100,000 range and more. They also attempt to revive the fortunes of long-dead artists whose work has fallen out of favor. They even work to make a market for the work of long-dead artists who never were in favor.

The arguments used by some dealers to sell old works that are now of small value, never were of value, and probably never will be of value should have a familiar ring to investors in penny stocks.

To keep the ball rolling, living artists, even relatively young ones, may form the subject of an announcement of a record price. Despite the fact that the auction tradition and the tradition at the grander art galleries favor dead artists, the works of some living artists for whom there are enough well-heeled enthusiasts may be the basis for an announcement.

Buying a living artist's work as investment is like grub-staking a prospector. Either is risky but acceptable if you don't overspend. Neither the artist nor the prospector is likely to have any real success.

Crass causes

What is usually ignored is the fact that one needs more than a masterpiece to generate an announcement of a record price. Inflation, particularly if combined with low interest rates, is a big help.

It also helps if the record-setting bidder's personal currency, such as the yen if the buyer is Japanese, has appreciated compared to the currency in which the art is being sold. It really isn't a big deal if a Japanese, whose currency may have appreciated 100% compared to the U.S. dollar, ends up paying 10% more in dollars than the last time the painting sold.

It is no accident that Europeans dominate the art markets when the Euro-currencies are strong. Japanese dominate, despite cultural differences, when the yen rises. And Americans buy everything in sight if the U.S. dollar is strong.

Currency movements can be a major factor in record prices. If an auction is held in yen instead of dollars, after the yen has appreciated, prices might fall. As a result, try to make purchases when the Canadian dollar is strong, and let others buy when the dollar is in the doldrums.

The penny paintings

Most new artists will not make it even if you like their work. Of course, if the promoter – the art dealer in this case – has a good track record, you may buy a few more so-called penny paintings or pay a bit more than otherwise. But unless you have good connections, it may be hard to buy into an attractive deal.

Otherwise, the pennies in art can be far more satisfying than the penny stocks issued in Vancouver. If you like the art and paid little for it, who really cares if it appreciates?

After the pennies come works by the juniors – local artists who have had a number of shows and who usually are represented by a reasonably prestigious dealer.

The work of a junior can cost well in excess of $10,000, but some good ones are available for around $5,000. It would be encouraging to say that the prices of these works will certainly appreciate – and some dealers say exactly that. But the truth is that the worth of most will dwindle. So if you buy a penny painting, make sure you like it as art.

Better dead than alive

Even junior artists who should be seniors mess up the deal if they stay alive. They can paint junk and sell works they should have burned, as was the case even with Picasso. In time, if the junior's work becomes blue chip, the world will be willing to distinguish between the good and the bad. But few juniors make that jump.

Canada's Norval Morrisseau is an excellent example of a junior who may come to nothing. Morrisseau is to woodland Indian painting what Van Gogh was to impressionist painting. Morrisseau has been awarded the Order of Canada and his works hang in every major museum in Canada, as well as abroad. Yet one can buy Morrisseau oils of good quality for much less than $10,000.

The trouble is that Morrisseau also shares Van Gogh's instability. He is extraordinarily self-destructive. He no longer has a permanent regular dealer. He falls into schemes that cheapen his art by resulting in too many poor reproductions of his work.

Except for these tragic weaknesses, Morrisseau could today be a painter of blue chip calibre. Will he be in any event? Who knows? Those who think so spend all they can on what they view as undervalued examples of his art. Others scratch their heads in wonder.

The risky blue chips

The blue chips – particularly Canadian blue chips – are generally bad investments.

Say you had bought a painting by Tom Thomson, the father of the Group of Seven, for $20 in 1918 and sold it for $35,000 in 1988. That rather handsome gain is a lot less impressive when translated into a compound rate of interest. In this case, the annual yield on the investment is 11.125%. Although that is somewhat better than the yield on most financial investments, it is a lot riskier.

Who, in 1918 or even 1928, would have recognized the commanding position painters like A.Y. Jackson, Casson and the other members of the Group of Seven would hold in Canada over the past two decades? Few investors did. Furthermore, converting a Thomson into cash during the Great Depression of the 1930s, when you might well have preferred cash to art, was virtually impossible. The return was not only risky; the investment was highly illiquid.

That's all behind us, so perhaps an investor should buy a Thomson today. Indeed, many investors are doing exactly that. The argument is that, ignoring fakes – a problem that grows in parallel with the prices of the artist's work – there won't be any more Thomsons painted. Furthermore, many of the holders, such as museums, will keep their Thomsons off the market. Thus, we really are dealing with a shrinking number of Thomsons. Still, it is not impossible to imagine a time when Thomson or the Group of Seven are viewed as simply regional examples of Post-Impressionism. Such a view could bring prices down appreciably.

Indeed, the only art that is truly of investment quality, comparable to government bonds or stocks of blue chip companies, are the best examples of the international masters. Their value is not distorted by regionalism because the works are well known and have been heavily reviewed. They have stood the test of time. If you cannot get top examples from the work of the 18th century masters, settle for those top drawer artists of the 19th century. But be careful of the 20th century; there is too much chance of trendiness that pushes prices above value. Who knows how Picasso's works will stand the test of real time?

Of course, most of us cannot afford the hundreds of thousands of dollars involved in buying a single example of such work. We may be decorating by buying works of imitators. We may be preening ourselves by buying low grade examples of the work of first class artists (a kind of autograph hunting). We may be showing off as art collectors. We may even really be collectors.

All of these things may be great fun. But they are not investing. Someone with limited dollars can get much better returns, albeit with less pleasure, in the securities markets.

CHAPTER SIXTEEN

TAX SHELTERS: EASING THE PAIN

EVERYONE LIKES TO KEEP TAXES TO A MINIMUM. INDEED, BECAUSE OF the way that taxation has increasingly bitten into incomes, cutting taxes has become a prime objective for many Canadians.

Tax avoidance – as opposed to tax evasion – is legal and involves the use of a variety of measures allowed by Ottawa to reduce taxes. For instance, RRSPs and pension plans are popular tax shelters. Investing in Canadian dividend-paying shares to get the dividend tax credit is another widely used method of cutting the amount you pay to Revenue Canada.

There are other ways people can shelter income, although some tax shelters are quite complex and not suitable for most families of moderate means. Moreover, the federal government has been cutting back on tax shelters. For example, in 1985 it virtually ended income-splitting plans between spouses and between parents and minor children. The most common strategy involved low-interest or no-interest loans between husbands and wives, whereby one spouse would lend funds to the other if the borrowing spouse had substantially lower income. The borrower would invest the funds and any interest earned would then be taxed at his or her marginal tax rate, which was usually much lower than that of the lending spouse.

With these spousal loans, families could circumvent Ottawa's attribution rules, which require that within a family, tax on investment income must be paid by the person who supplied the capital, not the person whose name is on the bank account or share certificates.

Although most income-splitting devices are gone, there are still some left. If one spouse makes a loan to the other to buy or invest in a business to be managed by the spouse to whom the money is lent, the profits are taxed in the hands of the spouse operating the business.

And you can still make low- or no-interest loans to children 18 and over for investment purposes. This make sense in the case of children attending university. With the loan, they can earn several thousand dollars of investment income that will be untaxed or lightly taxed because of their personal and tuition deductions. In effect, you've shifted investment income to be taxed at their marginal tax rates, which almost certainly will be lower than yours.

A shelter for education savings

As noted earlier, another shelter popular with parents who expect their children to attend university is the registered education savings plan (RESP). With an RESP, a parent or grandparent can shelter investment income from taxes, as long as the income is eventually used to finance post-secondary education expenses. You aren't entitled to a deduction for the funds that go into an RESP (you're allowed up to $30,000 per beneficiary), but interest earned and capital appreciation grows untaxed as long as it remains in the plan. Earnings are then taxable in the hands of the recipient when they are withdrawn. Several investment dealers and mutual fund management companies offer RESPs. As well, there are RESP "scholarship" plans.

There are some distinct disadvantages to RESPs. First, beneficiaries must go on to some sort of post-secondary education. If they don't, matters can get complicated and you may even lose a substantial amount of money. What happens to the earnings if beneficiaries decide not to continue their education depends on the type of RESP you have. The dealer-sponsored plans allow you to change beneficiaries if those you originally named decide not to continue beyond high school. With the scholarship plans, you forfeit the income earned on your capital and it is paid out to students who do continue their education.

The risk is always there

Other types of shelters allow individuals to invest in specific industries to reduce taxes. In return for investing in, say, mining exploration, Ottawa will allow you to deduct all or part of your investment from income for tax purposes. In some cases you may be able to deduct more than your actual investment, in which case the government is in effect subsidizing your investment with tax dollars.

Flow-through shares, for instance, have been behind the resurrection of the natural resource exploration industry in Canada. They have enabled companies to raise more than $1 billion for natural resource exploration and have in many cases been profitable for investors. Flow-throughs allow writeoffs that a mining company can't use (if it doesn't have profits) to flow through to the investor, who uses the writeoffs to reduce taxable income from other sources.

Flow-through shares, however, aren't for everyone. They usually make sense only for people paying the highest marginal tax rates and who, by virtue of their incomes, are best able to afford the risks involved. Moreover, individuals who are not paying the top marginal tax rate get a much smaller tax benefit from flow-throughs. In addition, your cumulative net investment losses (CNIL) must be considered if you haven't fully used your lifetime tax exemption. Ottawa will allow you to claim only that portion of your taxable lifetime capital gains exemption that exceeds your CNIL. You'll still be able to claim the unused portion of your exemption, but only when it exceeds your CNIL.

Another method of sheltering money from taxes is to invest with borrowed funds through a limited partnership in a venture that is losing money. You can write off your share of the losses from the limited partnership against other income and deduct the interest you pay for tax purposes. You are, of course, at risk for the money that you've borrowed. Ideally, the venture will eventually be sold and you will recover your after-tax costs or, better still, make a handsome profit.

The truth of the matter is that shelters are usually risky. However, some are a lot riskier than others and there are ways to separate those with good investment potential from those without. First, use the investment's prospectus to determine your after-tax costs. In other words, if you put up $10,000 and get $6,000 back from Ottawa, your after-tax cost is $4,000. Then determine – also from the prospectus – the after-tax value of the investment. For example, if you sold the shelter at the earliest possible time that allowed you a full tax writeoff, what would you get? If the value of your $4,000 investment (remember, you got $6,000 back from Ottawa) is, say, $5,000 after taxes when sold, it would appear to be a good prospect.

It is important to understand what you own when you buy a shelter and what that holding is worth. Too many investors have used borrowed money to buy a shelter, and then spent the tax refund while under the impression that the value of their investment was equal to the value of their loan. They then find that when it comes time to repay the loan, on liquidation of the investment, that the amount borrowed exceeded the after-tax value of the investment.

If you're in the market for tax shelters, you should look at the investment aspects of any proposal before you look at the tax implications. If it doesn't look good from an investment perspective, it should be avoided. The tax-shelter benefits should be considered the icing on the cake.

Marketability is another important factor. It is often quite difficult to get out of a shelter once you're in because in many cases there is no secondary market. The better shelters provide a mechanism for liquidity after a set period. For example, some flow-through limited partnerships roll into mutual funds that can be redeemed for full market value at any time. Others distribute the shares in which the partnership invests and these can be sold like other stocks.

In addition, you should be careful about how you finance your purchase. Interest on funds borrowed for investment is deductible for tax purposes, so many people have in the past borrowed to buy shelters in the hope of increasing their tax deductions and sheltering a major portion of their income from taxes. Problems arose when their investments failed to bring the promised returns and they found themselves in debt. What's more, if the shelter is sold or goes under, and you still owe money on it, the interest you pay will not be deductible.

Provincial stock savings plans

Some provinces have provincially sponsored tax shelters, the most successful and best known being the Quebec Stock Savings Plan. Introduced in 1979, the plan allows Quebec residents a tax break for investing in Quebec-based public companies.

The plan encourages Quebec residents to become investors rather than savers. As with any other investment, the tax aspect is an added bonus. Any shares considered should be able to stand on their own as investments.

CHAPTER SEVENTEEN

STRATEGIES: DO WHAT WORKS WELL

YOU MIGHT HAVE HEARD A LONG-TERM INVESTOR DESCRIBED AS "A short-term investor whose stock went down." There's some truth to this. Indeed, many people make the mistake of holding their losers indefinitely in the hope that they will rise in price. Sometimes the losers do recover, but those holding investments that have lost value should ask whether they can do better deploying capital elsewhere.

That's what this chapter is about: demonstrating some of the strategies you can use to structure your investments to meet your objectives and make the most of your money.

It pays to diversify

Strategy number one is diversification – in other words, don't put all your eggs in one basket. It's a fact of financial life that if you put everything in one security and the company has difficulties, you have serious problems as well. And putting all your money into a company you think is stable can also be a recipe for disaster; even blue-chip companies can have problems. You might recall when Massey-Ferguson was considered a blue-chip stock and paid handsome dividends – before it fell on hard times.

Of course, by diversifying you won't make the killing in the market that you would if you put everything in one stock that happens to skyrocket. But steady growth is preferable to watching your fortune go down the tubes.

Just how much you diversify depends on how much risk you are willing to take. Even splitting your money between two growth investments significantly reduces risk, so try to introduce some variety into your holdings or at least place a limit on the portion of your assets with which you speculate.

Another point worthy of consideration is diversification across different classes of assets. Many people diversify within one asset group, such as the stock market. But not venturing outside that asset group can be a mistake; no single class of asset is best all the time. Take the stock market as an example. Although it performed extremely well in the five years prior to the October 1987 crash, if you had all your money in the market during the crash you took a short-term beating. Similarly, there have been times when guaranteed investment certificates and long-term bonds have been poor investments, and periods when treasury bills have been a costly choice because of falling interest rates.

By spreading your investments among different types of assets – such as gold, interest income, dividend income, stocks and real estate – your returns are likely to be more stable than if you put everything in one growth-investment sector.

Manage your investments

Another secret to success is managing your investments well. To achieve maximum returns, you must constantly re-evaluate your holdings in light of current and anticipated economic and market conditions. For example, long-term government bonds may be safe, but you don't want to hold them if it looks like interest rates are ready to skyrocket. And you don't want a heavy equity position when stocks in general are a poor value relative to other investments.

Be prepared to change the mix of assets you hold to take advantage of opportunities while preserving capital. You must constantly monitor your individual holdings within asset groups to ensure each security continues to meet your criteria for holding on to that investment.

Even if you've delegated the management of your assets to a professional – through mutual funds, for instance – you must be aware of their status so you can determine whether your manager's performance is satisfactory. However, don't be too quick to make changes. You may want to judge professional results over a few years, or even a full market cycle, rather than over a couple of months.

Taxes and speculation

To make the most of your investments, any strategy must take full advantage of government approved methods of saving to meet specific objectives. Your RRSP, for instance, is the best way to save for retirement because of associated tax breaks

You should also keep the speculative portion of your portfolio within limits. There is nothing wrong with speculating, but it should only be done with money you can afford to lose. Don't, for example, gamble with your retirement prospects by speculating with your RRSP funds. Don't speculate if the loss of the funds involved will affect your lifestyle and destroy your chances of meeting other financial objectives.

How an investment of $1,000 a year can grow over time at different rates of return

YEARS	1%	2%	3%	4%	5%	6%	7%	8%	9%	10%
1	1,010	1,020	1,030	1,040	1,050	1,060	1,070	1,080	1,090	1,100
2	2,030	2,060	2,091	2,122	2,153	2,184	2,215	2,246	2,278	2,310
3	3,060	3,122	3,184	3,246	3,310	3,375	3,440	3,506	3,573	3,641
4	4,101	4,204	4,309	4,416	4,526	4,637	4,751	4,867	4,985	5,105
5	5,152	5,308	5,468	5,633	5,802	5,975	6,153	6,336	6,523	6,716
6	6,214	6,434	6,662	6,898	7,142	7,394	7,654	7,923	8,200	8,487
7	7,286	7,583	7,892	8,214	8,549	8,897	9,260	9,637	10,028	10,436
8	8,369	8,755	9,159	9,583	10,027	10,491	10,978	11,488	12,021	12,579
9	9,462	9,950	10,464	11,006	11,578	12,181	12,816	13,487	14,193	14,937
10	10,567	11,169	11,808	12,486	13,207	13,972	14,784	15,645	16,560	17,531
11	11,683	12,412	13,192	14,026	14,917	15,870	16,888	17,977	19,141	20,384
12	12,809	13,680	14,618	15,627	16,713	17,882	19,141	20,495	21,953	23,523
13	13,947	14,974	16,086	17,292	18,599	20,015	21,550	23,215	25,019	26,975
14	15,097	16,293	17,599	19,024	20,579	22,276	24,129	26,152	28,361	30,772
15	16,258	17,639	19,157	20,825	22,657	24,673	26,888	29,324	32,003	34,950
16	17,430	19,012	20,762	22,698	24,840	27,213	29,840	32,750	35,974	39,545
17	18,615	20,412	22,414	24,645	27,132	29,906	32,999	36,450	40,301	44,599
18	19,811	21,841	24,117	26,671	29,539	32,760	36,379	40,446	45,018	50,159
19	21,019	23,297	25,870	28,778	32,066	35,786	39,995	44,762	50,160	56,275
20	22,239	24,783	27,676	30,969	34,719	38,993	43,865	49,423	55,765	63,002
21	23,472	26,299	29,537	33,248	37,505	42,392	48,006	54,457	61,873	70,403
22	24,716	27,845	31,453	35,618	40,430	45,996	52,436	59,893	68,532	78,543
23	25,973	29,422	33,426	38,083	43,502	49,816	57,177	65,765	75,790	87,497
24	27,243	31,030	35,459	40,646	46,727	53,865	62,249	72,106	83,701	97,347
25	28,526	32,671	37,553	43,312	50,113	58,156	67,676	78,954	92,324	108,182
26	29,821	34,344	39,710	46,084	53,669	62,706	73,484	86,351	101,723	120,100
27	31,129	36,051	41,931	48,968	57,403	67,528	79,698	94,339	111,968	133,210
28	32,450	37,792	44,219	51,966	61,323	72,640	86,347	102,966	123,135	147,631
29	33,785	39,568	46,575	55,085	65,439	78,058	93,461	112,283	135,308	163,494
30	35,133	41,379	49,003	58,328	69,761	83,802	101,073	122,346	148,575	180,943
31	36,494	43,227	51,503	61,701	74,299	89,890	109,218	133,214	163,037	200,138
32	37,869	45,112	54,078	65,210	79,064	96,343	117,933	144,951	178,800	221,252
33	39,258	47,034	56,730	68,858	84,067	103,184	127,259	157,627	195,982	244,477
34	40,660	48,994	59,462	72,652	89,320	110,435	137,237	171,317	214,711	270,024
35	42,077	50,994	62,276	76,598	94,836	118,121	147,913	186,102	235,125	298,127
36	43,508	53,034	65,174	80,702	100,628	126,268	159,337	202,070	257,376	329,039
37	44,953	55,115	68,159	84,970	106,710	134,904	171,561	219,316	281,630	363,043
38	46,412	57,237	71,234	89,409	113,095	144,058	184,640	237,941	308,066	400,448
39	47,886	59,402	74,401	94,026	119,800	153,762	198,635	258,057	336,882	441,593
40	49,375	61,610	77,663	98,827	126,840	164,048	213,610	279,781	368,292	486,852

APPENDIX A

YEARS	11%	12%	13%	14%	15%	16%	17%	18%	19%	20%
1	1,110	1,120	1,130	1,140	1,150	1,160	1,170	1,180	1,190	1,200
2	2,342	2,374	2,407	2,440	2,473	2,506	2,539	2,572	2,606	2,640
3	3,710	3,779	3,850	3,921	3,993	4,066	4,141	4,215	4,291	4,368
4	5,228	5,353	5,480	5,610	5,742	5,877	6,014	6,154	6,297	6,442
5	6,913	7,115	7,323	7,536	7,754	7,977	8,207	8,442	8,683	8,930
6	8,783	9,089	9,405	9,730	10,067	10,414	10,772	11,142	11,523	11,916
7	10,859	11,300	11,757	12,233	12,727	13,240	13,773	14,327	14,902	15,499
8	13,164	13,776	14,416	15,085	15,786	16,519	17,285	18,086	18,923	19,799
9	15,722	16,549	17,420	18,337	19,304	20,321	21,393	22,521	23,709	24,959
10	18,561	19,655	20,814	22,045	23,349	24,733	26,200	27,755	29,404	31,150
11	21,713	23,133	24,650	26,271	28,002	29,850	31,824	33,931	36,180	38,581
12	25,212	27,029	28,985	31,089	33,352	35,786	38,404	41,219	44,244	47,497
13	29,095	31,393	33,883	36,581	39,505	42,672	46,103	49,818	53,841	58,196
14	33,405	36,280	39,417	42,842	46,580	50,660	55,110	59,965	65,261	71,035
15	38,190	41,753	45,672	49,980	54,717	59,925	65,649	71,939	78,850	86,442
16	43,501	47,884	52,739	58,118	64,075	70,673	77,979	86,068	95,022	104,931
17	49,396	54,750	60,725	67,394	74,836	83,141	92,406	102,740	114,266	127,117
18	55,939	62,440	69,749	77,969	87,212	97,603	109,285	122,414	137,166	153,740
19	63,203	71,052	79,947	90,025	101,444	114,380	129,033	145,628	164,418	185,688
20	71,265	80,699	91,470	103,768	117,810	133,841	152,139	173,021	196,847	224,026
21	80,214	91,503	104,491	119,436	136,632	156,415	179,172	205,345	235,438	270,031
22	90,148	103,603	119,205	137,297	158,276	182,601	210,801	243,487	281,362	325,237
23	101,174	117,155	135,831	157,659	183,168	212,978	247,808	288,494	336,010	391,484
24	113,413	132,334	154,620	180,871	211,793	248,214	291,105	341,603	401,042	470,981
25	126,999	149,334	175,850	207,333	244,712	289,088	341,763	404,272	478,431	566,377
26	142,079	168,374	199,841	237,499	282,569	336,502	401,032	478,221	570,522	680,853
27	158,817	189,699	226,950	271,889	326,104	391,503	470,378	565,481	680,112	818,223
28	177,397	213,583	257,583	311,094	376,170	455,303	551,512	668,447	810,523	983,068
29	198,021	240,333	292,199	355,787	433,745	529,312	646,439	789,948	965,712	1,180,882
30	220,913	270,293	331,315	406,737	499,957	615,162	757,504	933,319	1,150,387	1,418,258
31	246,324	303,848	375,516	464,820	576,100	714,747	887,449	1,102,496	1,370,151	1,703,109
32	274,529	341,429	425,463	531,035	663,666	830,267	1,039,486	1,302,125	1,631,670	2,044,931
33	305,837	383,521	481,903	606,520	764,365	964,270	1,217,368	1,537,688	1,942,877	2,455,118
34	340,590	430,663	545,681	692,573	880,170	1,119,713	1,425,491	1,815,652	2,313,214	2,947,341
35	379,164	483,463	617,749	790,673	1,013,346	1,300,027	1,668,994	2,143,649	2,753,914	3,538,009
36	421,982	542,599	699,187	902,507	1,166,498	1,509,191	1,953,894	2,530,686	3,278,348	4,246,811
37	469,511	608,831	791,211	1,029,998	1,342,622	1,751,822	2,287,225	2,987,389	3,902,424	5,097,373
38	522,267	683,010	895,198	1,175,338	1,545,165	2,033,273	2,677,224	3,526,299	4,645,075	6,118,048
39	580,826	766,091	1,012,704	1,341,025	1,778,090	2,359,757	3,133,522	4,162,213	5,528,829	7,342,858
40	645,827	859,142	1,145,486	1,529,909	2,045,954	2,738,478	3,667,391	4,912,591	6,580,496	8,812,629

APPENDIX B

The future value of a single deposit of $1,000 using different rates of return

YEARS	1%	2%	3%	4%	5%	6%	7%	8%	9%	10%
1	1,010	1,020	1,030	1,040	1,050	1,060	1,070	1,080	1,090	1,100
2	1,020	1,040	1,061	1,082	1,103	1,124	1,145	1,166	1,188	1,210
3	1,030	1,061	1,093	1,125	1,158	1,191	1,225	1,260	1,295	1,331
4	1,041	1,082	1,126	1,170	1,216	1,262	1,311	1,360	1,412	1,464
5	1,051	1,104	1,159	1,217	1,276	1,338	1,403	1,469	1,539	1,611
6	1,062	1,126	1,194	1,265	1,340	1,419	1,501	1,587	1,677	1,772
7	1,072	1,149	1,230	1,316	1,407	1,504	1,606	1,714	1,828	1,949
8	1,083	1,172	1,267	1,369	1,477	1,594	1,718	1,851	1,993	2,144
9	1,094	1,195	1,305	1,423	1,551	1,689	1,838	1,999	2,172	2,358
10	1,105	1,219	1,344	1,480	1,629	1,791	1,967	2,159	2,367	2,594
11	1,116	1,243	1,384	1,539	1,710	1,898	2,105	2,332	2,580	2,853
12	1,127	1,268	1,426	1,601	1,796	2,012	2,252	2,518	2,813	3,138
13	1,138	1,294	1,469	1,665	1,886	2,133	2,410	2,720	3,066	3,452
14	1,149	1,319	1,513	1,732	1,980	2,261	2,579	2,937	3,342	3,797
15	1,161	1,346	1,558	1,801	2,079	2,397	2,759	3,172	3,642	4,177
16	1,173	1,373	1,605	1,873	2,183	2,540	2,952	3,426	3,970	4,595
17	1,184	1,400	1,653	1,948	2,292	2,693	3,159	3,700	4,328	5,054
18	1,196	1,428	1,702	2,026	2,407	2,854	3,380	3,996	4,717	5,560
19	1,208	1,457	1,754	2,107	2,527	3,026	3,617	4,316	5,142	6,116
20	1,220	1,486	1,806	2,191	2,653	3,207	3,870	4,661	5,604	6,727
21	1,232	1,516	1,860	2,279	2,786	3,400	4,141	5,034	6,109	7,400
22	1,245	1,546	1,916	2,370	2,925	3,604	4,430	5,437	6,659	8,140
23	1,257	1,577	1,974	2,465	3,072	3,820	4,741	5,871	7,258	8,954
24	1,270	1,608	2,033	2,563	3,225	4,049	5,072	6,341	7,911	9,850
25	1,282	1,641	2,094	2,666	3,386	4,292	5,427	6,848	8,623	10,835
26	1,295	1,673	2,157	2,772	3,556	4,549	5,807	7,396	9,399	11,918
27	1,308	1,707	2,221	2,883	3,733	4,822	6,214	7,988	10,245	13,110
28	1,321	1,741	2,288	2,999	3,920	5,112	6,649	8,627	11,167	14,421
29	1,335	1,776	2,357	3,119	4,116	5,418	7,114	9,317	12,172	15,863
30	1,348	1,811	2,427	3,243	4,322	5,743	7,612	10,063	13,268	17,449
31	1,361	1,848	2,500	3,373	4,538	6,088	8,145	10,868	14,462	19,194
32	1,375	1,885	2,575	3,508	4,765	6,453	8,715	11,737	15,763	21,114
33	1,389	1,922	2,652	3,648	5,003	6,841	9,325	12,676	17,182	23,225
34	1,403	1,961	2,732	3,794	5,253	7,251	9,978	13,690	18,728	25,548
35	1,417	2,000	2,814	3,946	5,516	7,686	10,677	14,785	20,414	28,102
36	1,431	2,040	2,898	4,104	5,792	8,147	11,424	15,968	22,251	30,913
37	1,445	2,081	2,985	4,268	6,081	8,636	12,224	17,246	24,254	34,004
38	1,460	2,122	3,075	4,439	6,385	9,154	13,079	18,625	26,437	37,404
39	1,474	2,165	3,167	4,616	6,705	9,704	13,995	20,115	28,816	41,145
40	1,489	2,208	3,262	4,801	7,040	10,286	14,974	21,725	31,409	45,259

APPENDIX B

YEARS	11%	12%	13%	14%	15%	16%	17%	18%	19%	20%
1	1,110	1,120	1,130	1,140	1,150	1,160	1,170	1,180	1,190	1,200
2	1,232	1,254	1,277	1,300	1,323	1,346	1,369	1,392	1,416	1,440
3	1,368	1,405	1,443	1,482	1,521	1,561	1,602	1,643	1,685	1,728
4	1,518	1,574	1,630	1,689	1,749	1,811	1,874	1,939	2,005	2,074
5	1,685	1,762	1,842	1,925	2,011	2,100	2,192	2,288	2,386	2,488
6	1,870	1,974	2,082	2,195	2,313	2,436	2,565	2,700	2,840	2,986
7	2,076	2,211	2,353	2,502	2,660	2,826	3,001	3,185	3,379	3,583
8	2,305	2,476	2,658	2,853	3,059	3,278	3,511	3,759	4,021	4,300
9	2,558	2,773	3,004	3,252	3,518	3,803	4,108	4,435	4,785	5,160
10	2,839	3,106	3,395	3,707	4,046	4,411	4,807	5,234	5,695	6,192
11	3,152	3,479	3,836	4,226	4,652	5,117	5,624	6,176	6,777	7,430
12	3,498	3,896	4,335	4,818	5,350	5,936	6,580	7,288	8,064	8,916
13	3,883	4,363	4,898	5,492	6,153	6,886	7,699	8,599	9,596	10,699
14	4,310	4,887	5,535	6,261	7,076	7,988	9,007	10,147	11,420	12,839
15	4,785	5,474	6,254	7,138	8,137	9,266	10,539	11,974	13,590	15,407
16	5,311	6,130	7,067	8,137	9,358	10,748	12,330	14,129	16,172	18,488
17	5,895	6,866	7,986	9,276	10,761	12,468	14,426	16,672	19,244	22,186
18	6,544	7,690	9,024	10,575	12,375	14,463	16,879	19,673	22,901	26,623
19	7,263	8,613	10,197	12,056	14,232	16,777	19,748	23,214	27,252	31,948
20	8,062	9,646	11,523	13,743	16,367	19,461	23,106	27,393	32,429	38,338
21	8,949	10,804	13,021	15,668	18,822	22,574	27,034	32,324	38,591	46,005
22	9,934	12,100	14,714	17,861	21,645	26,186	31,629	38,142	45,923	55,206
23	11,026	13,552	16,627	20,362	24,891	30,376	37,006	45,008	54,649	66,247
24	12,239	15,179	18,788	23,212	28,625	35,236	43,297	53,109	65,032	79,497
25	13,585	17,000	21,231	26,462	32,919	40,874	50,658	62,669	77,388	95,396
26	15,080	19,040	23,991	30,167	37,857	47,414	59,270	73,949	92,092	114,475
27	16,739	21,325	27,109	34,390	43,535	55,000	69,345	87,260	109,589	137,371
28	18,580	23,884	30,633	39,204	50,066	63,800	81,134	102,967	130,411	164,845
29	20,624	26,750	34,616	44,693	57,575	74,009	94,927	121,501	155,189	197,814
30	22,892	29,960	39,116	50,950	66,212	85,850	111,065	143,371	184,675	237,376
31	25,410	33,555	44,201	58,083	76,144	99,586	129,946	169,177	219,764	284,852
32	28,206	37,582	49,947	66,215	87,565	115,520	152,036	199,629	261,519	341,822
33	31,308	42,092	56,440	75,485	100,700	134,003	177,883	235,563	311,207	410,186
34	34,752	47,143	63,777	86,053	115,805	155,443	208,123	277,964	370,337	492,224
35	38,575	52,800	72,069	98,100	133,176	180,314	243,503	327,997	440,701	590,668
36	42,818	59,136	81,437	111,834	153,152	209,164	284,899	387,037	524,434	708,802
37	47,528	66,232	92,024	127,491	176,125	242,631	333,332	456,703	624,076	850,562
38	52,756	74,180	103,987	145,340	202,543	281,452	389,998	538,910	742,651	1,020,675
39	58,559	83,081	117,506	165,687	232,925	326,484	456,298	635,914	883,754	1,224,810
40	65,001	93,051	132,782	188,884	267,864	378,721	533,869	750,378	1,051,668	1,469,772

■■■■■■■■■

APPENDIX C

Survey of Performance
of Canadian Mutual Funds
through June 30, 1988

This survey shows the per cent change in investment over three months, six months, and one year and the average annual compound rate of return over three years, five years and ten years. The column labeled "%" shows the percentile ranking by volatility within the grouping. For example, a percentile ranking of 5 for the fund means that 95% of the funds in the group are more volatile while 4% are less volatile. The column labeled "St.D" shows the standard deviation. This measure indicates the amount by which a fund's rate of return is likely to diverge from its average monthly rate of return. A fund with a standard deviation of 6 is twice as volatile as a fund with a standard deviation of 3.

Fund	3 mo.	6 mo.	1 yr.	3 yr.	5 yr.	10 yr.	%	St.D.
EQUITY FUNDS – RRSP ELIGIBLE								
AGF Excel Cdn Equity Fund	5.2	3.3	–	–	–	–	N/A	–
AIC Advantage Fund	6.8	1.5	-9.2	–	–	–	N/A	–
AMD Cdn Blue Chip Growth Fd	5.8	2.1	-9.4	–	–	–	N/A	–
All-Canadian Compound Fund	1.3	2.4	-9.3	6.9	8.4	13.6	28	3.77
All-Canadian Dividend Fund	1.3	2.3	-9.3	6.8	8.1	13.3	27	3.77
Allied Canadian Fund	4.8	-2.9	-28.6	–	–	–	N/A	–
Associate Investors Ltd.	4.7	4.9	-0.3	9.6	12.9	15.7	26	3.53
Bolton Tremblay Cda Cum Fund	7.0	4.3	-7.7	6.9	6.0	13.1	46	4.26
Bolton Tremblay Cdn Balanced	3.6	2.6	–	–	–	–	N/A	–
Bolton Tremblay Discovery	2.3	0.8	–	–	–	–	N/A	–
Bullock Growth Fund	7.3	3.3	-6.0	9.6	3.6	11.2	86	5.20
CDA RSP Balanced Fund	4.0	2.5	0.5	10.6	11.1	–	6	2.07
CDA RSP Common Stock Fund	8.6	4.5	-4.9	13.6	14.1	16.2	55	4.48
CGF Fund 4000	4.0	0.9	-13.4	7.8	8.6	11.4	79	4.92
CGF Venture Fund	4.7	2.0	-20.2	-9.8	-5.7	1.9	99	6.97
CMA Investment Fund	6.1	6.1	6.1	15.5	16.1	17.8	26	3.53
Caisse de Sec du Spectacle	2.5	1.8	-0.4	8.7	9.2	–	14	2.57
Cambridge Balanced Fund	1.1	1.4	6.9	15.1	14.1	12.8	5	2.03
Cambridge Growth Fund	4.8	4.1	-0.4	20.9	18.3	15.6	32	3.92
Cambridge Resource Fund	5.4	8.5	-7.7	11.5	8.9	10.4	96	6.30
Canadian Gas & Energy Fund Ltd	2.4	0.8	-15.5	6.6	0.8	9.5	97	6.45
Canadian Investment Fund Ltd.	5.7	3.0	-7.8	5.7	7.3	12.1	57	4.53
Canadian Natural Resource Fd	1.6	0.0	-14.3	–	–	–	N/A	–
Canadian Protected Fund	0.5	1.3	9.4	12.1	–	–	2	1.59
Canadian Security Growth Fund	5.1	3.5	-7.0	9.8	13.0	17.8	38	4.10
Capital Growth Fund Ltd.	5.9	4.2	-13.5	4.1	5.4	14.7	67	4.73
Capstone Investment Trust	5.5	1.2	-10.6	7.0	8.4	–	77	4.85
Cda Life Bal Eqty Income E-2	8.0	6.0	0.3	13.3	14.1	17.3	73	4.81
Cda Life Cdn & Intl Equity S-9	8.6	5.8	1.7	12.5	13.1	16.4	51	4.40

Fund	3 mo.	6 mo.	1 yr.	3 yr.	5 yr.	10 yr.	%	St.D.
Cda Life Managed Fund S-35	4.8	3.5	3.5	11.4	–	–	15	2.73
Cdn Anaesthetists Mutual Accum	8.1	4.5	-3.7	12.2	11.8	18.6	36	4.02
Cdn Convertible Preferred Fd	3.4	2.7	1.2	–	–	–	N/A	–
Cdn Gen Life Ins Equity Fd A	3.0	0.7	-9.7	9.2	12.1	16.8	56	4.51
Chou RRSP Fund	3.1	2.9	7.1	–	–	–	N/A	–
Confed Dolphin Fund	6.0	4.9	-3.4	11.9	12.8	17.1	33	3.97
Corporate Investors Ltd.	4.7	2.9	-3.0	6.7	9.9	12.4	23	3.19
Corporate Investors Stock Fund	3.2	-1.3	-31.4	3.8	6.8	14.2	84	5.15
Counsel Trust Real Estate Fd	0.5	1.8	13.7	16.4	–	–	1	1.52
Crown Life Commitment Fund	5.3	1.7	-4.7	–	–	–	N/A	–
Crown Life Pensions Balanced	2.8	2.1	2.9	–	–	–	N/A	–
Crown Life Pensions Equity	5.5	2.6	-3.6	13.1	11.6	13.0	52	4.44
Cundill Security Fund	3.8	3.9	2.1	11.3	12.1	–	20	3.13
DK All Seasons Fund	3.8	2.2	-16.9	3.0	-1.2	8.3	94	6.15
DK Enterprise Fund	0.4	-4.1	-10.8	12.8	4.2	14.0	91	5.71
Dynamic Fund of Canada Ltd.	4.1	3.6	-1.9	12.3	10.2	15.5	29	3.80
Dynamic Managed Portfolio	1.7	1.9	-2.3	–	–	–	N/A	–
Dynamic Precious Metals Fund	-0.8	0.8	-7.2	14.0	–	–	97	6.37
Empire Life Segregated #1	9.3	7.8	3.5	14.3	12.3	18.6	59	4.55
Ethical Growth Fund	7.9	3.9	12.3	–	–	–	N/A	–
Everest Balanced Fund	4.4	8.3	–	–	–	–	N/A	–
Everest Special Equity Fund	3.2	0.1	-19.5	–	–	–	N/A	–
F.M.O.Q. Fonds de Placement	5.1	4.2	-0.8	11.3	–	–	24	3.38
F.M.O.Q. Omnibus	4.1	3.7	2.9	11.8	12.0	–	9	2.24
Fd Des Prof Du Que-Balanced	1.2	1.6	–	–	–	–	N/A	–
Ficadre Actions	6.5	2.1	-13.4	10.6	–	–	80	4.94
Ficadre Equilibre	5.1	3.0	-3.7	8.2	–	–	16	2.81
Fidelity Cap Balanced Fund	5.2	5.9	–	–	–	–	N/A	–
Fidelity Cap Conservation Fd	5.8	6.5	–	–	–	–	N/A	–
Fidelity Cap. Builder Fund	6.5	6.5	–	–	–	–	N/A	–
Fiducie Pret Revenu Retraite	2.1	1.6	-1.4	8.3	9.1	10.8	8	2.15
Fiducie Pret Revenue Canadien	4.9	1.4	-14.8	3.7	3.8	8.9	68	4.74
First City Growth Fund	5.6	1.3	-9.2	–	–	–	N/A	–
First City Realfund	0.9	6.5	16.2	14.1	12.6	–	3	1.64
Fonds Desjardins Actions	5.7	3.7	-11.0	4.0	4.7	12.3	58	4.53
Fonds Desjardins Equilibre	2.4	2.1	-0.6	–	–	–	N/A	–
FoodFund	0.8	1.5	-9.4	9.3	–	–	25	3.42
Global Strategy Corp	-4.0	-3.5	-17.2	–	–	–	N/A	–
Global Strategy RRSP	2.8	2.6	–	–	–	–	N/A	–
Global Strategy RRSP Access	2.3	2.1	–	–	–	–	N/A	–
GoldenFund	-3.1	-3.0	-14.1	15.5	–	–	92	5.89
Green Line Cdn Index Fund	6.3	4.5	-6.2	–	–	–	N/A	–
Growth Equity Fund Ltd.	4.8	8.9	-17.0	10.0	8.3	16.3	89	5.51
Guardian Balanced Fund	4.9	3.5	5.9	10.6	12.8	13.5	7	2.13
Guardian Cdn Equity Fd	7.8	3.9	-7.6	12.5	10.2	14.6	83	5.11
Guardian Enterprise Fund	6.3	1.8	-1.9	10.0	10.6	17.7	79	4.92
Hallmark Canadian Fund	1.4	1.5	-4.2	12.2	–	–	22	3.19
Hume Canadian Equity Fund	8.0	6.8	–	–	–	–	N/A	–
Hume RRSP Growth&Income Fund	4.5	2.3	-14.3	5.3	–	–	75	4.83
Imperial Realty Growth Fund	1.4	1.4	10.3	15.4	–	–	4	1.89

Fund	3 mo.	6 mo.	1 yr.	3 yr.	5 yr.	10 yr.	%	St.D.
Industrial Dividend Fund Ltd.	8.5	9.3	6.1	16.3	17.4	17.1	65	4.69
Industrial Equity Fund Ltd.	5.8	4.4	-0.5	15.6	12.6	15.7	47	4.31
Industrial Future Fund	4.0	4.4	–	–	–	–	N/A	–
Industrial Growth Fund	6.2	6.8	4.5	15.8	15.2	17.9	35	4.01
Industrial Horizon Fund	5.4	6.0	15.2	–	–	–	N/A	–
Industrial Pension Fund	8.3	9.1	4.3	15.8	15.3	16.0	71	4.79
Integra Balanced Fund	3.0	3.3	–	–	–	–	N/A	–
Investors Cdn Equity Fund	6.6	6.8	-7.2	9.3	–	–	76	4.83
Investors Gr Tr Pooled Equity	6.2	5.0	-3.0	9.0	9.4	14.9	37	4.02
Investors Retirement Mutual	7.6	7.7	4.6	12.7	11.7	15.6	39	4.11
Investors Summa Fund Ltd	5.1	4.5	-3.1	–	–	–	N/A	–
Jones Heward Fund Ltd.	8.9	5.2	-3.9	11.6	11.5	17.0	85	5.20
Keltic Investment Trust	5.4	0.0	-10.1	9.2	4.9	–	54	4.45
LifeFund	0.0	-0.7	-17.3	4.8	–	–	31	3.86
London Life Diversified fund	4.7	3.6	–	–	–	–	N/A	–
London Life Equity Fund	9.6	6.3	-0.3	12.8	12.2	17.2	68	4.73
Lotus Fund	3.8	2.7	-6.1	7.4	–	–	21	3.14
MER Equity Fund	6.4	5.3	-6.0	10.1	12.6	–	48	4.31
MER Heartland Equity Fund	6.0	4.9	-7.1	–	–	–	N/A	–
MONY Balanced Fund	2.4	2.6	-0.9	–	–	–	N/A	–
MONY Canadian Growth Fund	4.0	3.0	-16.6	4.8	7.9	16.1	43	4.19
Mackenzie Equity Fund	8.0	8.3	4.8	15.9	15.8	19.2	60	4.59
Maritime Life Balanced Fund	4.4	2.9	1.9	–	–	–	N/A	–
Maritime Life Growth Fund	6.9	1.8	-11.1	8.5	10.8	14.9	64	4.63
Marlborough Fund	8.3	2.9	-16.0	5.5	5.7	12.6	88	5.50
Metropolitan Cdn Mutual Fd	6.0	5.1	-13.6	6.5	–	–	72	4.80
Metropolitan Growth Fund	3.3	1.6	-17.1	3.4	4.8	10.4	49	4.31
Metropolitan Var-Balanced Fd	2.1	0.3	-4.1	–	–	–	N/A	–
Metropolitan Variable-Equity	7.2	2.8	-11.8	–	–	–	N/A	–
Montreal Trust Equity Fund	7.0	4.2	-3.9	10.4	8.7	13.9	66	4.71
Morgan Growth Fund	7.4	0.0	-6.8	8.0	–	–	63	4.63
Morgan Resource Fund	7.7	4.9	7.0	–	–	–	N/A	–
Mtl Trust RRSP-Equity Sectn	6.1	1.2	-6.2	10.2	8.6	14.0	82	5.10
Multiple Opportunities Fund	-2.3	-6.0	-27.2	–	–	–	N/A	–
Mutual Canadian Index Fund	5.9	5.0	–	–	–	–	N/A	–
Mutual Diversifund 25	2.2	2.2	3.0	8.3	–	–	3	1.87
Mutual Diversifund 40	3.5	3.2	0.6	8.8	–	–	12	2.52
Mutual Diversifund 55	4.4	3.8	-1.0	8.9	–	–	18	2.97
Mutual Equifund	6.6	5.5	-6.2	8.6	–	–	78	4.88
NFM Canadian Equity Fund	7.6	-2.6	–	–	–	–	N/A	–
NW Canadian Fund Ltd.	6.3	4.9	-8.0	13.7	12.4	18.0	69	4.76
National Trust Cdn Common Shar	6.5	4.1	-3.5	12.7	11.7	15.7	70	4.77
National Trust Equity Fund	6.3	3.9	-9.7	8.9	9.8	15.0	85	5.19
Natl Trust Feb Pro Fund	4.3	3.0	0.9	10.8	–	–	13	2.55
Natl Trust Jan Pro Fund	5.2	1.5	4.6	10.2	–	–	15	2.72
Natural Resources Growth Fund	-0.4	0.2	-12.4	6.6	1.5	9.3	93	5.93
One Decision Fund	4.2	3.0	-4.6	–	–	–	N/A	–
Ont Teachers Grp Aggr Equity	4.8	4.3	-4.5	12.2	13.1	17.1	50	4.38

Fund	3 mo.	6 mo.	1 yr.	3 yr.	5 yr.	10 yr.	%	St.D.
Ont Teachers Grp Balanced	2.5	2.6	1.8	–	–	–	N/A	–
Ont Teachers Grp Diversified	4.2	4.0	-4.7	10.7	11.7	16.0	44	4.25
Ordre Ingenieurs Actions	7.5	4.4	-2.8	12.1	11.2	14.4	62	4.63
Ordre Ingenieurs Equilibre	4.0	3.6	2.8	11.8	11.9	–	10	2.34
PH&N Canadian Fund	6.2	4.7	-2.9	13.5	12.1	16.2	62	4.62
PH&N Pooled Pension Trust	6.5	3.7	-4.7	11.9	11.7	14.9	61	4.59
PH&N RRSP Fund	6.8	4.7	-6.3	12.1	11.1	14.3	74	4.81
Pacific Growth Fund	6.0	4.6	-10.8	5.0	3.0	10.4	90	5.60
Pacific Retirement Bal Fund	5.2	4.2	-3.0	4.8	5.0	–	19	3.05
Planned Resources Fund Ltd.	7.0	4.6	-14.0	4.4	2.6	13.7	95	6.29
Prudential Diversif Invstmt	2.8	2.1	–	–	–	–	N/A	–
Prudential Growth Fund Canada	4.1	1.2	-15.6	10.1	10.0	14.1	87	5.46
Prudential Nat Res Fd Of Cda	10.1	11.7	–	–	–	–	N/A	–
Prudential Precious Metals	-0.8	-0.7	–	–	–	–	N/A	–
Rabin Budden Capital Fund	5.1	4.0	-14.7	–	–	–	N/A	–
Rabin Budden Income Fund	2.4	6.9	13.1	–	–	–	N/A	–
Renaissance Cda Bond&Bullion	-6.9	-6.8	-6.9	–	–	11	2.40	
RoyFund Balanced Fund	3.2	3.6	–	–	–	–	N/A	
RoyFund Equity Ltd	5.2	2.3	-8.3	11.5	13.2	17.7	44	4.22
Royal Trust Adv Balanced Fd	3.2	2.5	0.3	–	–	–	N/A	–
Royal Trust Energy Fund	2.8	-0.3	-11.4	4.0	0.2	–	98	6.92
Saxon Balanced Fund	3.4	4.0	-13.1	–	–	–	N/A	–
Saxon Small Cap	2.2	2.8	-9.1	–	–	–	N/A	–
Saxon Stock Fund	3.3	3.3	-12.9	–	–	–	N/A	–
Sceptre Balanced Fund	4.3	2.7	3.4	–	–	–	N/A	–
Sceptre Equity fund	9.5	5.9	4.4	–	–	–	N/A	–
Scotia Stock And Bond Fund	1.8	2.2	4.8	–	–	–	N/A	–
Sentinel Cda Equity Fund	5.2	4.0	-13.0	–	–	–	N/A	–
SilverFund	-1.6	-3.7	-23.7	-0.7	–	–	100	9.01
Spectrum Canadian Equity Fd	3.7	2.5	-3.3	–	–	–	N/A	–
Spectrum Diversified Fund	2.4	2.0	1.6	–	–	–	N/A	–
St-Laurent Reer-Actions	6.0	2.1	-13.6	–	–	–	N/A	–
St-Laurent Reer-Diversifiee	2.1	1.5	5.0	–	–	–	N/A	–
Sunset Fund	3.6	3.6	1.7	–	–	–	N/A	–
Talvest Diversified Fund	5.5	4.2	4.6	–	–	–	N/A	–
Talvest Growth Fund	7.4	5.6	-1.8	13.0	12.3	14.6	41	4.13
TechnoFund	0.3	0.5	-19.8	-6.4	–	–	81	4.98
Templeton Canadian Fund	4.0	1.8	-11.4	9.1	7.1	–	53	4.44
Tradex Investment Fund Ltd.	7.9	4.6	-3.2	12.1	12.3	18.1	40	4.12
Trans-Canada Equity Fund	2.9	1.6	-1.0	22.4	19.7	15.7	32	3.91
Trans-Canada Shares Series C	1.7	1.3	3.5	16.4	16.5	14.1	17	2.90
Trimark Canadian Fund	5.2	6.1	1.6	12.8	13.3	–	50	4.35
Trimark Income Growth Fund	3.5	2.9	–	–	–	–	N/A	–
Trust General Balanced Fund	3.0	1.3	-0.2	–	–	–	N/A	–
Trust General Canadian Equity	8.3	2.7	-8.2	8.0	8.6	13.0	56	4.51
Trust La Laurentienne Action	5.8	3.9	-6.0	–	–	–	N/A	–
United Accumulative Retirement	3.3	3.1	-2.2	7.8	12.9	18.8	21	3.18
United Venture Retirement Fund	3.6	4.3	-9.8	9.7	10.7	18.9	38	4.07
Universal Svgs Equity Fund Ltd	8.3	8.4	11.0	17.4	16.5	18.4	45	4.25
Universal Svgs Natural Resourc	2.1	1.0	-4.1	8.6	5.2	11.2	91	5.66

Fund	3 mo.	6 mo.	1 yr.	3 yr.	5 yr.	10 yr.	%	St.D.
Univest Growth Fund	0.7	0.2	-7.9	7.4	7.2	11.0	30	3.81
ValueFund	2.1	1.9	-12.7	3.7	–	–	42	4.13
Viking Canadian Fund Ltd	5.7	5.1	-2.6	9.3	9.9	15.0	34	3.99
Vintage Fund	6.1	3.9	-10.2	–	–	–	N/A	–
Waltaine Balanced Fund	2.3	2.4	1.0	9.9	10.4	14.8	9	2.25
HIGHEST IN GROUP	10.1	11.7	16.2	22.4	19.7	19.2		
LOWEST IN GROUP	-6.9	-6.8	-31.4	-9.8	-5.7	1.9		
AVERAGE OF GROUP	4.4	3.1	-4.8	9.8	9.9	14.5		

EQUITY FUNDS – NOT RRSP-ELIGIBLE

Fund	3 mo.	6 mo.	1 yr.	3 yr.	5 yr.	10 yr.	%	St.D.
AGF Excel Amern Equity Fund	3.2	2.7	–	–	–	–	N/A	–
AGF HiTech Fund Ltd	-0.7	-2.8	-12.5	14.9	–	–	67	5.24
AGF Japan Fund Ltd.	-6.9	-8.8	4.6	38.6	30.4	21.7	89	5.79
AGF Option Equity Fund	-0.1	1.7	-11.2	1.8	5.5	–	7	3.38
AGF Special Fund Ltd.	5.4	4.9	-8.2	10.0	7.9	20.7	45	4.97
AMD Amer Blue Chip Growth Fd	2.9	5.1	-16.0	–	–	–	N/A	–
Allied International Fund	3.8	5.6	-27.7	–	–	–	N/A	–
American Growth Fund Ltd.	3.3	2.8	-15.0	5.4	8.0	17.2	51	5.09
Bolton Tremblay International	-0.1	0.6	-15.2	12.6	12.6	18.2	16	4.26
Bullock Amer Fund	4.4	2.6	-20.7	14.5	8.0	13.1	100	6.89
CGF Int'l Growth Fund	2.6	-0.5	-12.9	10.7	9.9	13.1	31	4.65
Cda Life U.S.&Intl Eqty S-34	3.9	2.3	-7.4	11.4	–	–	27	4.56
Century DJ Mutual Fund	2.8	-1.6	-25.6	–	–	–	N/A	–
Chou Associates Fund	4.1	2.5	-5.2	–	–	–	N/A	–
Crown Life Pen Foreign Equity	2.2	3.6	-6.0	12.4	11.9	–	35	4.71
Cundill Value Fund Ltd.	4.3	5.5	10.4	16.4	13.5	21.0	4	2.88
DK American Fund	1.5	-0.7	-23.4	2.7	1.5	10.1	93	5.86
Dynamic American Fund	1.9	2.4	-8.1	11.3	13.2	–	25	4.54
Dynamic Global Fund	-2.9	-2.4	-13.9	–	–	–	N/A	–
Everest International Fund	-3.1	1.0	–	–	–	–	N/A	–
Fidelity Intl Portfolio Fund	-1.7	-2.0	–	–	–	–	N/A	–
Fiducie Pret Revenu American	3.7	4.3	-22.3	6.6	7.7	10.5	69	5.28
Fonds Desjardins International	0.1	0.7	-17.0	9.2	7.7	11.2	53	5.09
G.T. Global Choice Fund	-1.9	-0.9	–	–	–	–	N/A	–
Global Strategy Americas	2.7	1.3	-18.0	–	–	–	N/A	–
Global Strategy Europe	-3.6	-4.9	-25.7	–	–	–	N/A	–
Global Strategy Far East	-5.7	-4.9	-8.8	–	–	–	N/A	–
Global Strategy Fund	-1.7	-3.0	-17.3	–	–	–	N/A	–
Green Line U.S. Fund	4.1	6.0	-7.8	–	–	–	N/A	–
Guardian American Eqty Fd	5.1	5.4	-13.1	3.9	1.6	12.1	44	4.96
Guardian Global Equity Fd	-4.0	-1.0	-13.9	13.9	10.4	15.7	29	4.59
Guardian North American Fund	4.3	6.2	-24.0	-0.8	-0.6	11.7	85	5.67
Guardian Pacific Rim Corp	-4.0	-2.6	–	–	–	–	N/A	–
Hume Growth & Income Fund	4.4	4.6	-23.7	4.6	–	–	96	6.14
Industrial American Fund	5.1	6.6	-6.3	11.9	12.5	18.0	49	5.07
Industrial Global Fund	1.6	0.9	-1.4	–	–	–	N/A	–
Investors Global Fund Ltd	-1.6	-1.3	-14.9	–	–	–	N/A	–
Investors Growth Fund of Cda	6.1	5.8	-9.8	10.4	9.8	15.6	33	4.67
Investors International Mutual	1.7	1.8	-14.4	8.3	7.3	13.3	75	5.51
Investors Japanese Growth Fund	-8.0	-9.6	4.5	37.3	26.0	19.1	78	5.62

Fund	3 mo.	6 mo.	1 yr.	3 yr.	5 yr.	10 yr.	%	St.D.
Investors Mutual of Canada Ltd	5.3	5.4	-1.9	9.4	8.4	13.7	11	3.75
Jones Heward American Fund	4.3	1.9	-17.5	9.5	10.1	–	76	5.57
London Life U.S. Equity Fund	5.1	3.7	–	–	–	–	N/A	–
MD Growth Investments Ltd.	2.8	5.1	-5.2	17.8	17.7	21.9	56	5.11
MD Perpetual Growth Fd II	0.4	-6.8	-20.9	–	–	–	N/A	–
MD Perpetual Growth Fund	0.4	0.6	3.8	–	–	–	N/A	–
MER Growth Fund	7.2	5.4	-15.9	0.8	5.2	–	62	5.14
MER Heartland Growth Fund	8.5	8.0	-14.7	–	–	–	N/A	–
Metropolitan Collective Mut	3.2	2.9	-27.7	-0.4	2.4	12.8	64	5.15
Metropolitan Speculators	1.5	-2.0	-20.6	–	–	–	N/A	–
Metropolitan Venture Fund	3.9	2.9	-21.6	7.7	4.2	11.9	71	5.36
Montreal Trust Intl Fund	4.5	4.7	-15.5	11.4	12.5	15.9	42	4.96
Morgan Worldwide Fund	2.4	0.6	-20.2	5.4	–	–	20	4.40
Mutual Amerifund	3.4	6.9	-3.6	–	–	–	N/A	–
NFM U.S. Equity Fund	5.0	10.1	–	–	–	–	N/A	–
NW Equity Fund Ltd.	9.2	7.0	-15.1	4.4	5.9	13.1	82	5.63
National Trust Pooled Non-Cdn	2.4	1.6	-14.5	10.9	8.2	13.1	80	5.63
Natl Trust Global Fund P	-2.7	-2.4	-17.7	20.6	18.3	–	36	4.85
Natrusco Common Share Fund	4.6	3.8	-12.5	7.5	7.2	12.6	47	5.07
Noram Convertible Securities	-0.2	0.6	3.9	12.4	–	–	0	2.16
PH&N U.S. FUND	5.8	6.4	-10.6	7.5	6.7	16.4	95	5.92
PH&N U.S. Pooled Pension Fund	5.9	6.8	-8.8	8.4	9.3	–	91	5.80
Pacific U.S. Growth Fund	2.8	4.3	-15.3	3.6	-0.1	5.9	87	5.69
Provident Stock Fund Ltd.	5.2	4.4	-10.0	8.4	4.3	14.3	55	5.10
Royal Trust A Fund	3.3	2.8	-15.6	9.1	6.9	11.7	40	4.94
Royal Trust Adv Growth Fund	3.4	2.5	-4.4	–	–	–	N/A	–
Royal Trust Global Invest	-4.0	-1.8	–	–	–	–	N/A	–
Royal Trust J Fund	-9.9	-12.1	-4.7	36.6	–	–	84	5.67
Salamander Trust	-1.9	-1.4	-4.9	5.0	–	–	5	2.93
Saxon World Growth	0.1	0.9	-10.8	–	–	–	N/A	–
Sceptre International Fund	5.2	7.7	-4.6	–	–	–	N/A	–
Sentinel Amer Fund	4.6	6.1	–	–	–	–	N/A	–
Sentinel Global Fund	-1.9	-3.6	-21.3	–	–	–	N/A	–
Spectrum Intl Equity Fund	-0.9	-2.8	-17.7	–	–	–	N/A	–
St-Laurent Placmt-Actions	10.3	5.3	–	–	–	–	N/A	–
Sunset World Fund	1.2	1.0	–	–	–	–	N/A	–
Talvest American Fund	5.6	5.1	-15.7	–	–	–	N/A	–
Taurus Fund Ltd.	5.2	3.8	-22.7	-1.1	0.7	13.4	73	5.37
Templeton Growth Fund	1.0	3.7	-10.4	12.1	14.0	17.0	15	4.25
Trans-Canada Shares Series B	2.5	2.3	8.9	19.5	17.8	14.4	2	2.72
Trimark Fund	4.8	9.6	-0.5	15.3	13.8	–	65	5.24
Trust General U.S. Equity	5.3	2.9	-20.9	9.4	7.8	–	60	5.13
United Accumulative Fund Ltd.	1.1	1.8	-14.9	8.5	13.4	18.1	13	4.25
United American Fund Ltd.	4.1	2.8	-17.3	5.2	10.4	14.0	22	4.40
United Venture Fund Ltd.	4.4	6.9	-18.5	2.7	6.5	15.9	38	4.90
Universal Savings American	3.3	5.3	-5.8	12.4	13.2	–	58	5.11
Universal Savings Global Fd	-1.4	-0.8	-11.4	–	–	–	N/A	–
Universal Savings Pacific Fd	-4.3	-3.7	-8.0	37.6	26.6	–	98	6.32
Universal Sector Canadian Fd	8.0	8.0	–	–	–	–	N/A	–

Fund	3 mo.	6 mo.	1 yr.	3 yr.	5 yr.	10 yr.	%	St.D.
Universal Sector Global Fund	-1.4	-1.0	–	–	–	–	N/A	–
Universal Sector Pacific Fd	-4.2	-3.7	–	–	–	–	N/A	–
Universal Sector Resource Sh	2.0	0.7	–	–	–	–	N/A	–
Universal Sectors Amer Fund	3.1	5.2	–	–	–	–	N/A	–
Viking Commonwealth Fund	2.8	2.8	-3.4	15.1	13.8	15.7	9	3.45
Viking Growth Fund Ltd	4.8	4.5	-8.5	14.4	13.2	15.0	18	4.35
Viking International Fund	3.5	3.4	-5.2	11.5	12.2	16.1	24	4.47
HIGHEST IN GROUP	10.3	10.1	10.4	38.6	30.4	21.9		
LOWEST IN GROUP	-9.9	-12.1	-27.7	-1.1	-0.6	5.9		
AVERAGE OF GROUP	1.9	1.9	-12.2	11.2	10.1	14.9		

BOND AND MORTGAGE FUNDS

Fund	3 mo.	6 mo.	1 yr.	3 yr.	5 yr.	10 yr.	%	St.D.
AGF Excel Cdn Bond Fund	1.4	1.8	–	–	–	–	N/A	–
AGF Global Government Bd Fd	-6.3	-8.2	1.6	–	–	–	N/A	–
AMD Fixed Income Fd	1.6	1.6	8.3	9.2	–	–	74	1.98
All-Canadian Revenue Grwth Fnd	0.9	1.5	6.6	7.2	9.3	11.1	24	1.13
Allied Income Fund	0.0	-4.6	5.9	–	–	–	N/A	–
Altamira Income Fund	1.4	1.9	10.4	9.9	10.8	11.8	40	1.32
Bolton Tremblay Bond & Mtg	1.8	2.9	–	–	–	–	N/A	–
Bullock Bond Fund	0.8	0.5	6.1	6.4	7.9	–	64	1.90
CDA RSP Fixed Income Fund	1.5	1.5	8.2	10.1	11.1	11.3	46	1.54
Canadian Trusteed Income Fund	1.5	1.8	7.4	11.0	13.2	11.9	98	2.51
Cda Life Fixed Income S-19	1.4	1.4	6.9	9.3	10.8	10.4	54	1.71
Cdn Convertible Debenture Fd	2.7	3.4	1.3	–	–	–	N/A	–
Cdn Gen Life Ins Security B	1.2	1.8	3.4	7.2	10.6	12.1	56	1.72
Confed Dolphin Mortgage Fund	-0.2	0.7	8.8	9.2	10.7	11.6	10	0.73
Crown Life Pensions Bond Fund	2.8	3.3	9.3	9.5	8.2	8.1	70	1.97
Crown Life Pensions Mortgage	0.6	0.8	8.6	10.1	11.9	11.0	26	1.16
Dynamic Income Fund	1.7	2.4	6.6	9.6	11.7	–	44	1.51
Everest Bond Fund	0.7	1.4	10.8	–	–	–	N/A	–
Fd Des Prof Du Que-Bonds	0.9	1.1	5.9	10.1	11.3	11.9	42	1.37
Ficadre Obligations	1.1	1.9	7.9	8.7	–	–	28	1.20
Fiducie Pret Revenu Fonds H	1.2	0.7	8.5	10.6	11.4	12.1	34	1.26
First Canadian Mortgage Fund	0.1	1.2	9.2	10.0	11.3	11.5	16	0.79
First City Income Fund	2.6	2.3	6.5	–	–	–	N/A	–
Fonds Desjardins Hypotheques	0.3	1.2	9.5	9.8	10.8	11.4	12	0.74
Guardian Strategic Income	-1.0	-0.4	5.1	–	–	–	N/A	–
Hallmark Bond Fund	1.2	1.9	8.9	10.6	–	–	72	1.97
Hume Canadian Bond Fund	1.1	2.1	–	–	–	–	N/A	–
Industrial Income Fund	3.0	3.2	13.2	14.7	15.7	11.2	68	1.92
Investors Bond Fund	1.5	1.8	7.4	10.0	11.3	–	82	2.12
Investors Gr Tr Fixed Income	0.6	1.7	9.5	10.4	11.7	11.3	18	0.81
Investors Group Trust Bond	1.7	2.1	9.4	11.6	12.6	–	80	2.11
Investors Mortgage Fund	0.4	1.5	8.8	9.5	10.7	11.2	14	0.77
London Life Bond Fund	2.3	2.0	5.3	10.0	13.9	12.1	100	3.09
London Life Mortgage Fund	0.1	1.9	8.7	10.5	11.8	10.7	36	1.30
MER Heartland Bond Fund	1.3	1.8	9.0	–	–	–	N/A	–
MONY Bond Fund	2.6	2.4	4.9	–	–	–	N/A	–

Fund	3 mo.	6 mo.	1 yr.	3 yr.	5 yr.	10 yr.	%	St.D.
Mackenzie Mortgage & Income Fu	3.4	3.9	13.0	14.3	15.2	13.3	58	1.76
Metropolitan Bond Fund	0.7	1.7	-3.2	5.8	7.5	–	88	2.18
Metropolitan Variable-Bond	-2.7	-2.6	2.1	–	–	–	N/A	–
Montreal Trust Income Fund	0.4	0.7	6.6	11.1	11.2	10.1	66	1.90
Montreal Trust Mortgage Fund	0.3	1.4	8.9	9.3	10.4	10.9	6	0.62
Morgan Income Fund	1.1	1.5	7.1	10.0	–	–	32	1.25
Mtl Trust RRSP-Income Sectn	0.9	0.7	6.7	10.8	11.5	10.8	52	1.70
Mtl Trust RRSP-Mortgage Sectn	0.3	1.3	8.5	9.1	10.2	10.7	4	0.59
National Trust Income Fund	1.3	1.8	7.8	10.4	11.3	10.5	78	2.09
National Trust Pooled Bond & Pr	1.4	2.1	8.3	10.2	11.4	11.1	62	1.89
National Trust Pooled Mortgage	1.2	2.3	11.3	11.1	11.9	12.2	2	0.57
Ordre Ingenieurs Obligations	1.2	1.5	6.3	9.9	11.3	10.2	60	1.80
PH&N Bond Fund	1.4	2.2	9.5	12.4	13.0	11.2	90	2.20
Protected Bond Fund	1.3	2.1	7.2	–	–	–	N/A	–
Prudential Income Fund Canada	1.4	2.1	9.3	9.9	11.3	10.7	30	1.21
RoyFund Bond Fund	1.1	1.8	7.8	10.0	10.8	10.5	50	1.65
Royal Trust Adv Income Fd	2.2	2.1	3.1	–	–	–	N/A	–
Royal Trust Bond Fund	1.4	1.7	7.3	9.9	11.8	10.9	84	2.15
Royal Trust Mortgage Fund	0.0	1.1	9.1	9.7	10.9	11.4	8	0.73
Sceptre Bond Fund	0.9	1.0	8.5	–	–	–	N/A	–
Scotia Income Fund	1.5	1.4	6.9	–	–	–	N/A	–
Sentinel Cda Bond Fund	0.5	0.9	6.5	–	–	–	N/A	–
Spectrum Interest Fund	1.0	1.5	6.0	–	–	–	N/A	–
St-Laurent Placmt-Obligatns	1.2	1.6	–	–	–	–	N/A	–
St-Laurent Reer-Obligations	1.4	1.2	7.9	–	–	–	N/A	–
Talvest Income Fund	1.0	2.1	8.1	9.0	10.3	11.4	22	0.91
Trst Laurentienne Obligation	2.3	1.5	6.4	–	–	–	N/A	–
Trust General Bond Fund	1.5	1.5	7.3	10.0	12.5	11.2	92	2.30
Trust General Mortgage Fund	-0.1	1.3	7.9	9.9	11.7	11.2	20	0.88
United Mortgage	0.5	1.9	7.9	8.1	9.7	10.7	0	0.48
United Security Fund	0.8	1.8	5.2	9.4	10.7	9.5	48	1.58
Universal Svgs Income Fund	1.7	1.9	12.1	11.5	12.7	10.5	96	2.42
Viking Income Fund	1.2	1.7	7.7	10.4	12.1	9.9	76	2.08
Waltaine Income Fund	1.2	2.1	2.8	–	–	–	N/A	–
HIGHEST IN GROUP	3.4	3.9	13.2	14.7	15.7	13.3		
LOWEST IN GROUP	-6.3	-8.2	-3.2	5.8	7.5	8.1		
AVERAGE OF GROUP	1.0	1.4	7.4	10.0	11.3	11.1		

PREFERRED DIVIDEND FUNDS

Fund	3 mo.	6 mo.	1 yr.	3 yr.	5 yr.	10 yr.	%	St.D.
AGF Preferred Income Fund	0.5	1.7	3.6	7.1	–	–	N/A	1.15
AMD Dividend Fund	0.9	0.8	1.5	5.4	–	–	N/A	1.26
Allied Dividend Fund	1.0	1.1	0.5	–	–	–	N/A	–
Bolton Tremblay Income Fund	2.1	2.7	3.1	6.8	7.6	9.7	N/A	1.48
Bullock Dividend Fund	2.8	1.9	0.0	5.6	–	–	N/A	2.20

Fund	3 mo.	6 mo.	1 yr.	3 yr.	5 yr.	10 yr.	%	St.D.
Sentinel Cda Money Market Fd	0.7	2.2	9.7	–	–	–	N/A	–
Spectrum Cash Reserve Fund	0.7	1.9	8.0	–	–	–	N/A	–
Spectrum Savings Fund	0.7	1.9	–	–	–	–	N/A	–
St-Laurent Placmt-Monetaire	0.7	1.8	–	–	–	–	N/A	–
St-Laurent Reer-Epargne-Plus	0.7	1.5	8.3	–	–	–	N/A	–
Talvest Money Fund	0.8	2.4	9.5	–	–	–	N/A	–
Trimark Interest Fund	0.7	2.1	8.6	–	–	–	N/A	–
Trust General Money Market	0.1	1.0	11.2	–	–	–	N/A	–
United Cdn Money Market Fund	0.8	2.2	–	–	–	–	N/A	–
United US$ Money Market Fund	0.6	1.8	–	–	–	–	N/A	–
Universal Sector Currency Fd	0.2	0.8	–	–	–	–	N/A	–
Viking Money Market Fund	0.7	2.1	8.4	8.9	–	–	N/A	0.09
Waltaine Instant MMF	1.3	2.7	–	–	–	–	N/A	–
HIGHEST IN GROUP	1.3	2.7	11.2	9.7	9.3	11.3		
LOWEST IN GROUP	-0.1	-0.4	4.0	6.6	7.6	10.5		
AVERAGE OF GROUP	0.6	1.8	8.1	8.3	8.8	10.9		
MARKET INDICES								
91 Day Canada T Bill	0.7	2.2	8.7	8.6	9.3	11.1		0.10
Consumer Price Index	0.6	1.5	4.1	4.3	4.3	6.9		0.23
MYW Weighted 50 Mid-Term Index	1.3	1.8	8.6	11.0	12.7	–		2.25
Standard & Poor's 500 Index	2.8	4.7	-15.3	12.2	14.2	17.2		5.04
TSE Total Return Index	6.2	4.7	-5.2	11.5	10.5	16.0		4.87

APPENDIX D

*Survey of Annual Rates of Return
of Canadian Mutual Funds
through June 30, 1988*

Fund	1988	1987	1986	1985	1984	1983	1982	1981	1980	1979
EQUITY FUNDS - RRSP-ELIGIBLE										
AIC Advantage Fund	-9.2	16.7	–	–	–	–	–	–	–	–
AMD Cdn Blue Chip Growth Fd	-9.4	13.3	–	–	–	–	–	–	–	–
All-Canadian Compound Fund	-9.3	15.3	16.8	18.3	3.8	26.9	4.8	39.1	8.3	19.5
All-Canadian Dividend Fund	-9.3	15.3	16.7	17.6	3.0	24.5	4.8	39.4	8.5	19.7
Allied Canadian Fund	-28.6	23.9	–	–	–	–	–	–	–	–
Associate Investors Ltd.	-0.3	14.9	15.0	33.7	4.2	74.6	-30.6	21.6	15.4	38.3
Bolton Tremblay Cda Cum Fund	-7.7	10.7	19.4	11.7	-2.0	80.0	-32.4	33.7	22.8	28.4
Bullock Growth Fund	-6.0	4.4	34.0	5.6	-14.2	75.3	-46.1	36.6	38.1	35.5
CDA RSP Balanced Fund	0.5	13.0	19.2	24.5	0.4	49.9	-22.7	8.7	-1.5	–
CDA RSP Common Stock Fund	-4.9	22.4	25.7	31.4	0.6	65.4	-21.5	12.8	14.5	38.1
CGF Fund 4000	-13.4	13.0	28.0	22.5	-1.4	35.9	-7.8	24.1	11.5	12.5
CGF Venture Fund	-20.2	15.2	-20.3	4.5	-2.5	28.5	-12.2	-2.6	14.3	28.4
CMA Investment Fund	6.1	20.5	20.5	33.9	2.3	62.0	-12.1	12.1	17.8	30.3
Caisse de Sec du Spectacle	-0.4	7.9	19.4	26.3	-4.1	43.9	1.3	11.4	–	–
Cambridge Balanced Fund	6.9	10.3	29.4	26.7	0.1	26.5	8.3	6.3	4.7	12.9
Cambridge Growth Fund	-0.4	26.3	40.7	31.5	-0.3	47.9	-16.9	27.2	-1.4	19.6
Cambridge Resource Fund	-7.7	27.5	17.9	10.6	-0.3	48.6	-13.4	0.2	11.2	23.1
Canadian Gas & Energy Fund Ltd	-15.5	69.4	-15.4	-3.5	-11.3	70.9	-52.4	10.2	56.8	69.3
Canadian Investment Fund Ltd.	-7.8	11.1	15.1	27.3	-5.1	66.4	-22.7	14.7	13.8	30.7
Canadian Natural Resource Fd	-14.3	–	–	–	–	–	–	–	–	–
Canadian Protected Fund	9.4	5.2	22.3	–	–	–	–	–	–	–
Canadian Security Growth Fund	-7.0	12.0	27.2	35.5	2.6	80.4	-31.5	31.8	21.7	40.9
Capital Growth Fund Ltd.	-13.5	18.6	10.0	26.2	-8.9	61.3	-11.5	20.4	25.6	40.7
Capstone Investment Trust	-10.6	10.1	24.6	26.9	-3.8	36.4	1.1	–	–	–
Cda Life Bal Eqty Income E-2	0.3	14.3	26.9	33.9	-0.6	65.7	-25.7	19.0	26.8	36.5
Cda Life Cdn&Intl Equity S-9	1.7	14.0	23.0	31.0	-1.0	64.3	-26.8	19.4	25.9	36.2
Cda Life Managed Fund S-35	3.5	11.4	20.0	27.4	–	–	–	–	–	–
Cdn Anaesthetists Mutual Accum	-3.7	20.4	21.7	27.2	-2.6	59.5	-25.3	30.4	30.8	54.4
Cdn Convertible Preferred Fd	1.2	14.3	–	–	–	–	–	–	–	–
Cdn Gen Life Ins Equity Fd A	-9.7	14.3	26.3	38.5	-1.8	58.3	-23.1	24.0	27.7	38.1
Chou RRSP Fund	7.1	–	–	–	–	–	–	–	–	–
Confed Dolphin Fund	-3.4	16.3	24.9	33.9	-2.6	74.6	-31.4	12.3	30.1	51.9
Corporate Investors Ltd.	-3.0	22.3	2.4	27.7	3.3	63.0	-21.9	17.6	8.5	24.3
Corporate Investors Stock Fund	-31.4	13.9	43.0	26.4	-1.5	81.2	-45.5	30.8	38.1	51.8
Counsel Trust Real Estate Fd	13.7	14.6	21.0	–	–	–	–	–	–	–

Fund	1988	1987	1986	1985	1984	1983	1982	1981	1980	1979
Crown Life Pen Foreign Equity	-6.0	19.2	26.7	31.1	-5.9	30.9	4.8	–	–	–
Cundill Value Fund Ltd.	10.4	16.5	22.4	13.5	5.5	66.7	0.0	40.0	6.6	43.2
DK American Fund	-23.4	9.2	29.4	34.1	-25.8	45.2	-21.6	29.9	30.9	25.2
Dynamic American Fund	-8.1	22.7	22.3	31.1	2.9	58.5	-11.1	39.7	–	–
Dynamic Global Fund	-13.9	–	–	–	–	–	–	–	–	–
Fiducie Pret Revenu American	-22.3	15.0	35.4	24.3	-3.5	37.0	-7.5	21.7	8.6	12.0
Global Strategy Fund	-17.3	24.7	–	–	–	–	–	–	–	–
Green Line U.S. Fund	-7.8	–	–	–	–	–	–	–	–	–
Guardian American Eqty Fd	-13.1	12.8	14.5	10.5	-12.7	41.1	-7.4	28.0	38.9	24.8
Guardian Global Equity Fd	-13.9	13.3	51.3	20.2	-7.6	39.1	-20.0	52.7	32.3	16.6
Guardian North American Fund	-24.0	3.1	24.7	13.1	-12.3	45.1	-1.6	29.0	34.6	25.9
Hume Growth & Income Fund	-23.7	3.2	45.3	–	–	–	–	–	–	–
Industrial American Fund	-6.3	18.4	26.3	29.9	-1.3	55.9	-5.1	38.9	14.8	23.3
Industrial Global Fund	-1.4	32.1	–	–	–	–	–	–	–	–
Investors Global Fund Ltd	-14.9	–	–	–	–	–	–	–	–	–
Investors Growth Fund of Cda	-9.8	18.8	25.5	28.5	-7.4	69.2	-23.7	15.7	28.5	38.9
Investors International Mutual	-14.4	18.5	25.3	27.2	-12.2	66.5	-14.8	23.7	25.2	12.2
Investors Japanese Growth Fund	4.5	31.8	87.9	7.2	14.4	34.3	-15.7	66.0	1.1	-4.8
Investors Mutual of Canada Ltd	-1.9	18.4	12.7	21.6	-5.9	68.6	-19.7	12.3	21.7	29.7
Jones Heward American Fund	-17.5	14.6	39.0	20.2	2.2	–	–	–	–	–
MD Growth Investments Ltd.	-5.2	25.8	36.9	37.2	0.7	74.3	-16.9	42.9	16.2	33.6
MD Perpetual Growth Fd II	-20.9	–	–	–	–	–	–	–	–	–
MD Perpetual Growth Fund	3.8	–	–	–	–	–	–	–	–	–
MER Growth Fund	-15.9	1.9	19.5	16.9	7.5	–	–	–	–	–
MER Heartland Growth Fund	-14.7	–	–	–	–	–	–	–	–	–
MONY Global Fund	-18.5	–	–	–	–	–	–	–	–	–
Metropolitan Collective Mut	-27.7	6.1	28.9	14.9	-1.0	60.0	-5.4	30.9	23.4	21.7
Metropolitan Speculators	-20.6	29.1	–	–	–	–	–	–	–	–
Metropolitan Venture Fund	-21.6	17.8	35.1	11.9	-12.0	45.7	-5.7	38.6	15.1	14.7
Montreal Trust Intl Fund	-15.5	18.7	37.8	36.2	-4.1	42.5	-1.8	23.3	13.5	23.8
Morgan Worldwide Fund	-20.2	13.1	29.9	11.2	–	–	–	–	–	–
Mutual Amerifund	-3.6	9.3	–	–	–	–	–	–	–	–
NW Equity Fund Ltd.	-15.1	6.3	26.1	26.6	-7.4	55.0	-5.5	29.1	15.4	17.4
National Trust Pooled Non-Cdn	-14.5	5.5	51.2	30.0	-16.3	45.8	5.4	27.8	6.5	10.0
Natl Trust Global Fund P	-17.7	26.5	68.6	19.5	10.4	–	–	–	–	–
Natrusco Common Share Fund	-12.5	17.0	21.3	18.1	-3.6	71.1	-29.1	19.8	14.1	40.2
Noram Convertible Securities	3.9	30.5	4.7	–	–	–	–	–	–	–
PH&N U.S. FUND	-10.6	8.1	28.8	32.4	-15.8	86.2	-4.2	38.8	14.8	16.3
PH&N U.S. Pooled Pension Fund	-8.8	8.7	28.7	33.4	-8.4	82.0	-3.6	–	–	–
Pacific U.S. Growth Fund	-15.3	11.0	18.2	12.4	-20.4	24.2	-15.4	22.2	21.4	14.3
Provident Stock Fund Ltd.	-10.0	16.6	21.3	17.7	-17.9	89.6	-30.2	25.2	35.2	37.6
Royal Trust A Fund	-15.6	16.8	31.8	21.9	-11.9	45.4	-5.6	22.9	11.1	15.5
Royal Trust Adv Growth Fund	-4.4	–	–	–	–	–	–	–	–	–
Royal Trust J Fund	-4.7	42.4	87.7	–	–	–	–	–	–	–
Salamander Trust	-4.9	-6.5	30.2	18.5	–	–	–	–	–	–

Fund	1988	1987	1986	1985	1984	1983	1982	1981	1980	1979
MER Heartland Equity Fund	-7.1	–	–	–	–	–	–	–	–	–
MONY Balanced Fund	-0.9	–	–	–	–	–	–	–	–	–
MONY Canadian Growth Fund	-16.6	20.3	14.6	34.9	-5.6	85.3	-17.3	17.5	26.2	33.8
Mackenzie Equity Fund	4.8	20.8	23.1	29.6	3.0	67.9	-26.8	25.7	25.1	44.6
Maritime Life Balanced Fund	1.9	–	–	–	–	–	–	–	–	–
Maritime Life Growth Fund	-11.1	15.2	24.7	34.8	-2.8	73.2	-30.9	15.1	24.7	40.1
Marlborough Fund	-16.0	13.7	23.0	25.5	-10.4	74.0	-32.3	17.2	20.5	48.5
Metropolitan Cdn Mutual Fd	-13.6	10.5	26.4	–	–	–	–	–	–	–
Metropolitan Growth Fund	-17.1	7.0	24.7	18.9	-4.1	54.7	-31.6	20.8	16.5	43.5
Metropolitan Var-Balanced Fd	-4.1	–	–	–	–	–	–	–	–	–
Metropolitan Variable-Equity	-11.8	–	–	–	–	–	–	–	–	–
Montreal Trust Equity Fund	-3.9	22.3	14.6	24.5	-9.6	66.1	-30.2	17.1	25.4	42.3
Morgan Growth Fund	-6.8	-4.7	41.8	24.5	–	–	–	–	–	–
Morgan Resource Fund	7.0	48.8	–	–	–	–	–	–	–	–
Mtl Trust RRSP-Equity Sectn	-6.2	21.0	17.7	25.0	-9.7	69.3	-29.5	17.2	24.8	40.5
Multiple Opportunities Fund	-27.2	93.5	–	–	–	–	–	–	–	–
Mutual Diversifund 25	3.0	6.4	15.9	–	–	–	–	–	–	–
Mutual Diversifund 40	0.6	6.8	19.7	–	–	–	–	–	–	–
Mutual Diversifund 55	-1.0	7.7	20.9	–	–	–	–	–	–	–
Mutual Equifund	-6.2	7.9	26.7	–	–	–	–	–	–	–
NW Canadian Fund Ltd.	-8.0	18.4	35.0	32.0	-7.4	83.8	-29.4	27.3	25.4	40.5
National Trust Cdn Common Shar	-3.5	18.6	25.0	25.9	-3.4	47.4	-20.3	19.3	24.5	41.4
National Trust Equity Fund	-9.7	14.6	24.9	31.0	-5.9	50.9	-20.5	19.9	25.3	40.7
Natl Trust Feb Pro Fund	0.9	13.3	18.9	7.5	–	–	–	–	–	–
Natl Trust Jan Pro Fund	4.6	8.8	17.7	8.0	–	–	–	–	–	–
Natural Resources Growth Fund	-12.4	50.3	-8.1	0.1	-11.1	41.6	-10.1	19.4	17.7	26.0
One Decision Fund	-4.6	10.3	–	–	–	–	–	–	–	–
Ont Teachers Grp Aggr Equity	-4.5	18.4	24.8	38.4	-5.4	75.3	-28.9	22.2	27.2	35.6
Ont Teachers Grp Balanced	1.8	13.3	–	–	–	–	–	–	–	–
Ont Teachers Grp Diversified	-4.7	17.3	21.3	34.7	-4.8	68.2	-26.6	18.6	26.9	35.8
Ordre Ingenieurs Actions	-2.8	23.7	17.0	30.8	-7.6	85.3	-37.6	24.1	23.9	27.2
Ordre Ingenieurs Equilibre	2.8	17.2	16.1	25.8	-0.5	51.6	-14.9	–	–	–
PH&N Canadian Fund	-2.9	16.1	29.7	28.1	-5.5	88.7	-40.9	36.5	25.4	33.0
PH&N Pooled Pension Trust	-4.7	18.7	23.8	28.6	-3.5	85.8	-34.6	19.7	24.3	27.9
PH&N RRSP Fund	-6.3	16.5	29.0	29.3	-7.2	95.3	-38.9	22.2	22.7	26.2
Pacific Growth Fund	-10.8	8.2	19.9	16.0	-13.7	67.8	-28.1	19.4	21.0	33.4
Pacific Retirement Bal Fund	-3.0	2.0	16.3	21.8	-8.9	50.7	-8.2	8.4	12.8	–
Planned Resources Fund Ltd.	-14.0	25.0	5.9	4.0	-3.9	73.3	-33.8	25.0	36.2	62.6
Prudential Growth Fund Canada	-15.6	27.9	23.7	27.9	-5.8	74.7	-35.5	14.8	24.3	44.5
Rabin Budden Capital Fund	-14.7	12.5	–	–	–	–	–	–	–	–
Rabin Budden Income Fund	13.1	12.6	–	–	–	–	–	–	–	–
Renaissance Cda Bond&Bullion	-6.9	2.6	4.8	–	–	–	–	–	–	–
RoyFund Equity Ltd	-8.3	12.1	34.9	35.2	-0.9	82.1	-40.7	24.4	37.6	48.1
Royal Trust Adv Balanced Fd	0.3	–	–	–	–	–	–	–	–	–
Royal Trust Cdn Stock Fund	-5.7	17.8	11.3	24.6	-8.6	79.0	-34.1	14.6	28.8	43.3
Royal Trust Energy Fund	-11.4	66.6	-23.7	0.1	-10.3	39.2	-41.8	–	–	–
Saxon Balanced Fund	-13.1	4.5	–	–	–	–	–	–	–	–
Saxon Small Cap	-9.1	11.8	–	–	–	–	–	–	–	–
Saxon Stock Fund	-12.9	5.5	–	–	–	–	–	–	–	–
Sceptre Balanced Fund	3.4	13.4	–	–	–	–	–	–	–	–

Fund	1988	1987	1986	1985	1984	1983	1982	1981	1980	1979
Sceptre Equity fund	4.4	–	–	–	–	–	–	–	–	–
Scotia Stock And Bond Fund	4.8	–	–	–	–	–	–	–	–	–
Sentinel Cda Equity Fund	-13.0	22.4	–	–	–	–	–	–	–	–
SilverFund	-23.7	53.2	-16.3	–	–	–	–	–	–	–
Spectrum Canadian Equity Fd	-3.3	–	–	–	–	–	–	–	–	–
Spectrum Diversified Fund	1.6	–	–	–	–	–	–	–	–	–
St-Laurent Reer-Actions	-13.6	16.4	–	–	–	–	–	–	–	–
St-Laurent Reer-Diversifiee	5.0	8.1	–	–	–	–	–	–	–	–
Sunset Fund	1.7	10.9	–	–	–	–	–	–	–	–
Talvest Diversified Fund	4.6	18.3	–	–	–	–	–	–	–	–
Talvest Growth Fund	-1.8	27.2	15.4	27.5	-2.8	52.8	-29.8	40.6	5.7	37.3
TechnoFund	-19.8	-5.3	8.1	–	–	–	–	–	–	–
Templeton Canadian Fund	-11.4	19.0	23.0	20.9	-10.1	–	–	–	–	–
Tradex Investment Fund Ltd.	-3.2	20.1	21.1	26.1	0.4	62.4	-26.2	27.6	24.7	55.1
Trans-Canada Equity Fund	-1.0	26.1	47.0	34.2	-0.3	54.0	-25.5	15.6	8.2	22.0
Trans-Canada Shares Series C	3.5	16.9	30.3	32.4	2.7	27.7	-3.8	17.8	5.3	14.1
Trimark Canadian Fund	1.6	19.6	18.1	31.5	-0.9	85.1	–	–	–	–
Trust General Balanced Fund	-0.2	–	–	–	–	–	–	–	–	–
Trust General Canadian Equity	-8.2	14.8	19.7	26.1	-4.9	63.5	-36.2	17.6	23.7	48.0
Trust La Laurentienne Action	-6.0	13.4	–	–	–	–	–	–	–	–
United Accumulative Retirement	-2.2	4.8	22.3	42.9	2.4	54.4	-29.0	28.0	28.1	69.4
United Venture Retirement Fund	-9.8	13.7	28.9	31.9	-4.5	66.9	-40.5	36.1	43.7	74.7
Universal Svgs Equity Fund Ltd	11.0	17.1	24.3	31.1	1.3	54.4	-13.4	12.2	17.4	43.0
Universal Svgs Natural Resourc	-4.1	51.2	-11.7	4.3	-3.6	81.6	-39.2	2.1	53.2	30.2
Univest Growth Fund	-7.9	10.2	22.1	20.7	-5.3	35.6	-12.2	35.9	8.4	14.7
ValueFund	-12.7	6.9	19.4	–	–	–	–	–	–	–
Viking Canadian Fund Ltd	-2.6	11.1	20.6	25.9	-2.4	66.8	-29.8	19.2	26.6	42.4
Vintage Fund	-10.2	25.1	–	–	–	–	–	–	–	–
Waltaine Balanced Fund	1.0	13.3	16.0	21.9	1.5	37.1	1.6	7.7	25.2	28.3
HIGHEST IN GROUP	16.2	93.5	50.7	42.9	7.8	95.3	8.3	40.6	67.1	21.5
LOWEST IN GROUP	-31.4	-12.8	-23.7	-3.5	-18.4	24.5	-52.4	-39.8	-2.4	12.5
AVERAGE OF GROUP	-4.8	17.9	19.8	23.6	-3.4	63.3	-24.5	18.8	22.8	38.0

EQUITY FUNDS – NOT RRSP-ELIGIBLE

Fund	1988	1987	1986	1985	1984	1983	1982	1981	1980	1979
AGF HiTech Fund Ltd	-12.5	18.7	46.2	-0.1	–	–	–	–	–	–
AGF Japan Fund Ltd.	4.6	31.8	92.9	15.9	22.6	32.4	-21.0	57.0	11.2	3.4
AGF Option Equity Fund	-11.2	6.0	12.0	25.5	-1.3	29.8	3.0	19.8	–	–
AGF Special Fund Ltd.	-8.2	10.5	31.2	23.4	-10.9	96.1	-12.6	50.6	33.2	30.7
AMD Amer Blue Chip Growth Fd	-16.0	12.6	–	–	–	–	–	–	–	–
Allied International Fund	-27.7	47.0	–	–	–	–	–	–	–	–
American Growth Fund Ltd.	-15.0	8.4	27.0	33.3	-6.0	62.9	-5.3	43.2	27.9	17.6
Bolton Tremblay International	-15.2	19.5	41.1	25.4	1.1	67.6	-9.2	45.5	12.9	17.2
Bullock Amer Fund	-20.7	21.2	56.0	16.8	-16.2	62.6	-16.0	46.4	17.9	-0.9
CGF Int'l Growth Fund	-12.9	13.7	37.2	14.4	3.4	30.3	1.5	45.5	-3.0	14.4
Cda Life U.S.&Intl Eqty S-34	-7.4	13.3	31.7	27.8	–	–	–	–	–	–
Century DJ Mutual Fund	-25.6	14.3	–	–	–	–	–	–	–	–
Chou Associates Fund	-5.2	–	–	–	–	–	–	–	–	–

Fund	1988	1987	1986	1985	1984	1983	1982	1981	1980	1979
Crown Life Commitment Fund	-4.7	–	–	–	–	–	–	–	–	–
Crown Life Pensions Balanced	2.9	11.0	–	–	–	–	–	–	–	–
Crown Life Pensions Equity	-3.6	18.2	26.9	36.0	-12.1	53.6	-28.1	12.3	13.3	39.7
Cundill Security Fund	2.1	22.6	10.3	24.2	3.4	57.1	-24.5	16.8	–	–
DK All Seasons Fund	-16.9	-12.8	50.7	-0.3	-13.5	42.5	-35.7	31.5	23.6	57.7
DK Enterprise Fund	-10.8	19.8	34.4	4.8	-18.4	68.7	-36.9	15.4	40.1	75.2
Dynamic Fund of Canada Ltd.	-1.9	25.3	15.2	23.0	-6.5	65.2	-31.1	23.7	26.8	45.2
Dynamic Managed Portfolio	-2.3	30.0	–	–	–	–	–	–	–	–
Dynamic Precious Metals Fund	-7.2	73.2	-7.9	1.1	–	–	–	–	–	–
Empire Life Segregated #1	3.5	16.9	23.5	31.9	-9.4	85.9	-26.0	37.3	22.6	33.6
Ethical Growth Fund	12.3	9.1	–	–	–	–	–	–	–	–
Everest Special Equity Fund	-19.5	–	–	–	–	–	–	–	–	–
F.M.O.Q. Fonds de Placement	-0.8	23.3	12.7	21.4	–	–	–	–	–	–
F.M.O.Q. Omnibus	2.9	17.5	15.6	25.1	0.7	42.4	4.6	5.9	–	–
Ficadre Actions	-13.4	19.4	31.0	–	–	–	–	–	–	–
Ficadre Equilibre	-3.7	14.7	14.9	–	–	–	–	–	–	–
Fiducie Pret Revenu Retraite	-1.4	11.1	16.0	17.2	3.6	44.5	-7.9	-1.5	10.8	24.9
Fiducie Pret Revenue Canadien	-14.8	17.8	11.1	12.2	-3.8	78.4	-35.6	8.8	15.5	34.7
First City Growth Fund	-9.2	–	–	–	–	–	–	–	–	–
First City Realfund	16.2	11.4	14.6	13.2	7.8	–	–	–	–	–
Fonds Desjardins Actions	-11.0	8.7	16.2	24.9	-10.4	76.2	-29.0	20.9	20.6	39.6
Fonds Desjardins Equilibre	-0.6	–	–	–	–	–	–	–	–	–
FoodFund	-9.4	5.6	36.6	–	–	–	–	–	–	–
Global Strategy Corp	-17.2	24.9	–	–	–	–	–	–	–	–
GoldenFund	-14.1	55.2	15.5	–	–	–	–	–	–	–
Green Line Cdn Index Fund	-6.2	23.3	–	–	–	–	–	–	–	–
Growth Equity Fund Ltd.	-17.0	20.3	33.2	21.5	-7.6	90.9	-49.8	27.4	53.8	61.2
Guardian Balanced Fund	5.9	14.7	11.5	29.8	3.8	50.3	-5.6	3.8	10.4	19.9
Guardian Cdn Equity Fd	-7.6	14.5	34.5	23.6	-7.7	59.7	-24.4	18.4	29.6	30.1
Guardian Enterprise Fund	-1.9	8.9	24.4	24.4	0.2	86.9	-24.6	23.0	36.4	30.6
Hallmark Canadian Fund	-4.2	12.7	30.9	–	–	–	–	–	–	–
Hume RRSP Growth&Income Fund	-14.3	12.5	21.2	–	–	–	–	–	–	–
Imperial Realty Growth Fund	10.3	24.9	11.5	7.0	–	–	–	–	–	–
Industrial Dividend Fund Ltd.	6.1	27.4	16.5	33.2	6.5	69.7	-21.4	16.8	-1.3	40.8
Industrial Equity Fund Ltd.	-0.5	31.4	18.1	16.8	0.3	88.1	-25.4	10.5	20.2	27.1
Industrial Growth Fund	4.5	27.7	16.4	27.1	2.8	77.7	-17.1	8.6	24.9	28.1
Industrial Horizon Fund	15.2	–	–	–	–	–	–	–	–	–
Industrial Pension Fund	4.3	23.4	20.8	30.6	0.6	84.0	-21.2	11.6	-2.4	37.4
Investors Cdn Equity Fund	-7.2	10.1	27.9	25.5	–	–	–	–	–	–
Investors Gr Tr Pooled Equity	-3.0	15.7	15.4	27.0	-4.8	64.9	-27.0	16.4	26.7	43.8
Investors Real Property Fund	8.2	10.0	10.0	9.8	–	–	–	–	–	–
Investors Retirement Mutual	4.6	20.4	13.6	26.7	-3.9	58.3	-27.0	15.8	27.9	42.7
Investors Summa Fund Ltd	-3.1	–	–	–	–	–	–	–	–	–
Jones Heward Fund Ltd.	-3.9	11.8	29.4	31.6	-5.7	73.8	-34.7	31.4	26.4	47.4
Keltic Investment Trust	-10.1	12.0	29.4	9.6	-10.9	78.9	-39.4	-39.8	67.1	–
LifeFund	-17.3	10.1	26.6	–	–	–	–	–	–	–
London Life Equity Fund	-0.3	21.0	19.0	28.7	-3.8	65.3	-21.3	15.7	26.4	44.0
Lotus Fund	-6.1	10.4	19.6	25.7	–	–	–	–	–	–
MER Equity Fund	-6.0	15.4	23.2	25.6	7.7	–	–	–	–	–

Fund	1988	1987	1986	1985	1984	1983	1982	1981	1980	1979
Saxon World Growth	-10.8	31.6	–	–	–	–	–	–	–	–
Sceptre International Fund	-4.6	–	–	–	–	–	–	–	–	–
Sentinel Global Fund	-21.3	–	–	–	–	–	–	–	–	–
Spectrum Intl Equity Fund	-17.7	–	–	–	–	–	–	–	–	–
Talvest American Fund	-15.7	17.8	–	–	–	–	–	–	–	–
Taurus Fund Ltd.	-22.7	1.1	23.8	11.9	-4.3	58.2	-9.9	57.9	25.4	20.7
Templeton Growth Fund	-10.4	19.3	31.8	28.1	6.7	56.2	-14.0	28.3	16.7	24.2
Trans-Canada Shares Series B	8.9	19.8	30.9	28.1	3.6	36.2	-12.0	12.4	4.4	20.5
Trimark Fund	-0.5	17.5	31.2	26.5	-1.6	82.8	–	–	–	–
Trust General U.S. Equity	-20.9	18.3	39.9	29.6	-14.1	–	–	–	–	–
United Accumulative Fund Ltd.	-14.9	11.7	34.3	32.7	10.6	39.8	-17.9	30.5	27.9	46.8
United American Fund Ltd.	-17.3	6.3	32.3	29.2	9.3	38.7	-10.0	36.2	11.1	19.9
United Venture Fund Ltd.	-18.5	4.3	27.4	30.3	-3.1	55.5	-31.5	38.8	40.5	53.9
Universal Savings American	-5.8	18.9	26.8	27.6	2.5	37.4	4.2	61.5	-3.5	–
Universal Savings Global Fd	-11.4	19.0	–	–	–	–	–	–	–	–
Universal Savings Pacific Fd	-8.0	34.8	110.0	13.2	10.1	23.4	–	–	–	–
Viking Commonwealth Fund	-3.4	21.2	30.4	24.3	0.7	55.0	-7.7	30.9	4.7	14.5
Viking Growth Fund Ltd	-8.5	15.2	42.3	27.6	-2.6	50.7	-17.3	32.2	10.0	19.8
Viking International Fund	-5.2	10.4	32.4	21.1	6.0	54.2	-14.5	54.5	5.5	16.5
HIGHEST IN GROUP	10.4	47.0	110.0	37.2	22.6	96.1	5.4	66.0	40.5	53.9
LOWEST IN GROUP	-27.7	-6.5	4.7	-0.1	-25.8	23.4	-31.5	12.3	-3.5	-4.8
AVERAGE OF GROUP	-12.2	16.5	35.8	22.7	-3.3	53.1	-10.6	35.0	17.3	21.8
BOND AND MORTGAGE FUNDS										
AGF Global Government Bd Fd	1.6	–	–	–	–	–	–	–	–	–
AMD Fixed Income Fd	8.3	4.7	14.7	–	–	–	–	–	–	–
All-Canadian Revenue Grwth Fnd	6.6	9.0	6.1	20.0	5.5	22.5	11.3	8.2	8.4	14.9
Allied Income Fund	5.9	16.1	–	–	–	–	–	–	–	–
Altamira Income Fund	10.4	7.5	11.8	21.8	3.2	26.8	13.8	3.9	11.4	9.2
Bullock Bond Fund	6.1	4.0	9.2	11.0	9.3	10.7	6.8	-2.5	11.8	–
CDA RSP Fixed Income Fund	8.2	8.1	14.0	21.2	4.8	32.2	15.3	-0.7	5.7	7.3
Canadian Trusteed Income Fund	7.4	5.8	20.4	31.4	3.5	31.2	18.4	-3.9	3.1	7.2
Cda Life Fixed Income S-19	6.9	6.4	14.8	24.7	2.5	37.0	12.8	-4.6	2.4	6.7
Cdn Convertible Debenture Fd	1.3	12.0	–	–	–	–	–	–	–	–
Cdn Gen Life Ins Security B	3.4	2.9	15.9	31.8	1.6	40.7	-4.9	7.7	12.4	16.6
Confed Dolphin Mortgage Fund	8.8	8.4	10.4	17.1	8.8	25.4	15.4	4.4	9.9	8.5
Crown Life Pensions Bond Fund	9.3	3.9	15.7	20.1	-6.0	33.6	7.5	-5.9	1.6	6.9
Crown Life Pensions Mortgage	8.6	8.6	13.2	21.7	7.8	38.4	15.8	-6.9	3.7	4.6
Dynamic Income Fund	6.6	8.2	14.1	30.3	1.5	36.3	6.4	-2.0	–	–
Everest Bond Fund	10.8	–	–	–	–	–	–	–	–	–
Fd Des Prof Du Que-Bonds	5.9	8.7	15.9	21.5	5.4	29.7	14.8	1.3	11.8	7.3
Ficadre Obligations	7.9	8.1	10.2	–	–	–	–	–	–	–
Fiducie Pret Revenu Fonds H	8.5	12.5	10.7	17.5	7.9	23.8	19.4	5.3	8.3	8.2
First Canadian Mortgage Fund	9.2	9.2	11.5	18.4	8.5	21.4	18.3	3.3	8.7	8.2
First City Income Fund	6.5	–	–	–	–	–	–	–	–	–
Fonds Desjardins Hypotheques	9.5	8.8	11.2	18.9	5.8	25.1	17.3	3.6	7.6	8.1

Fund	1988	1987	1986	1985	1984	1983	1982	1981	1980	1979
Fonds Desjardins Obligations	7.1	5.4	15.9	29.8	-3.2	37.6	13.7	-14.1	0.5	5.7
Guardian Strategic Income	5.1	–	–	–	–	–	–	–	–	–
Hallmark Bond Fund	8.9	7.0	16.1	–	–	–	–	–	–	–
Industrial Income Fund	13.2	12.3	18.6	38.0	-0.5	39.0	5.9	-7.0	-5.0	7.3
Investors Bond Fund	7.4	6.4	16.3	28.5	0.0	28.3	13.7	-7.7	-1.1	–
Investors Gr Tr Fixed Income	9.5	9.3	12.4	20.4	7.1	27.4	15.1	0.7	5.4	7.7
Investors Group Trust Bond	9.4	8.3	17.4	29.5	0.6	30.8	14.4	-5.8	-1.5	–
Investors Mortgage Fund	8.8	8.4	11.4	18.5	7.0	23.8	16.7	3.7	7.6	7.4
London Life Bond Fund	5.3	4.2	21.2	41.3	2.0	31.6	13.5	-1.9	3.8	7.3
London Life Mortgage Fund	8.7	9.3	13.7	22.9	5.3	41.9	15.5	-10.0	1.6	5.3
MER Heartland Bond Fund	9.0	–	–	–	–	–	–	–	–	–
MONY Bond Fund	4.9	–	–	–	–	–	–	–	–	–
Mackenzie Mortgage & Income Fu	13.0	12.5	17.6	30.3	4.3	27.6	14.2	0.9	8.0	8.0
Metropolitan Bond Fund	-3.2	7.9	13.3	27.1	-4.8	31.4	2.3	-3.1	0.0	–
Metropolitan Variable-Bond	2.1	–	–	–	–	–	–	–	–	–
Montreal Trust Income Fund	6.6	7.7	19.5	25.1	-0.8	35.0	11.4	-7.1	2.7	6.7
Montreal Trust Mortgage Fund	8.9	8.2	10.7	16.6	7.7	20.2	17.5	5.2	8.3	6.9
Morgan Income Fund	7.1	6.5	16.5	20.6	–	–	–	–	–	–
Mtl Trust RRSP-Income Sectn	6.7	8.2	17.9	23.1	2.8	43.6	9.5	-7.1	3.2	7.0
Mtl Trust RRSP-Mortgage Sect	8.5	8.2	10.5	16.4	7.6	19.9	17.0	5.2	8.1	6.8
National Trust Income Fund	7.8	7.3	16.3	30.0	-2.3	43.0	9.6	-7.7	2.6	7.1
National Trust Pooled Bond &Pr	8.3	5.7	17.0	26.3	1.4	33.5	13.4	-3.2	5.7	7.5
National Trust Pooled Mortgage	11.3	10.0	12.2	15.3	10.9	21.9	18.9	5.2	8.7	8.3
Ordre Ingenieurs Obligations	6.3	8.4	15.3	26.2	1.8	45.7	13.9	-13.0	-0.6	8.0
PH&N Bond Fund	9.5	9.4	18.6	34.0	-3.2	44.8	9.0	-8.9	0.3	8.4
Protected Bond Fund	7.2	3.1	–	–	–	–	–	–	–	–
Prudential Income Fund Canada	9.3	7.3	13.3	22.6	4.9	32.1	11.7	-0.9	3.0	6.9
RoyFund Bond Fund	7.8	6.8	15.7	23.9	1.0	23.4	8.6	0.9	13.3	6.5
Royal Trust Adv Income Fd	3.1	–	–	–	–	–	–	–	–	–
Royal Trust Bond Fund	7.3	6.2	16.5	30.0	1.3	35.5	11.7	-2.1	1.3	7.3
Royal Trust Mortgage Fund	9.1	8.7	11.3	16.8	8.6	20.8	18.7	5.2	7.9	8.3
Sceptre Bond Fund	8.5	7.4	–	–	–	–	–	–	–	–
Scotia Income Fund	6.9	–	–	–	–	–	–	–	–	–
Sentinel Cda Bond Fund	6.5	8.0	–	–	–	–	–	–	–	–
Spectrum Interest Fund	6.0	–	–	–	–	–	–	–	–	–
St-Laurent Reer-Obligations	7.9	7.4	–	–	–	–	–	–	–	–
TD's Green Line Mtge Fund	9.7	8.5	10.5	13.7	8.7	22.1	18.3	5.7	8.8	7.6
Talvest Bond Fund	7.9	9.3	16.0	30.2	2.5	40.7	12.3	-0.2	5.2	8.9
Talvest Income Fund	8.1	8.6	10.3	19.1	5.8	22.3	16.6	7.1	9.4	7.9
Trst Laurentienne Obligation	6.4	9.5	–	–	–	–	–	–	–	–
Trust General Bond Fund	7.3	5.4	17.8	32.9	1.6	31.9	14.3	-3.5	2.3	8.2
Trust General Mortgage Fund	7.9	9.1	12.7	21.7	7.7	23.9	17.1	1.0	4.7	8.5
United Mortgage	7.9	7.6	8.9	15.0	9.2	14.8	17.6	6.6	11.3	8.7
United Security Fund	5.2	8.1	15.0	27.0	-0.1	21.9	11.4	0.9	2.8	6.4
Universal Svgs Income Fund	12.1	7.0	15.7	36.4	-3.7	50.8	7.9	-11.7	-1.6	5.7
Viking Income Fund	7.7	7.3	16.5	30.9	0.5	37.9	10.9	-8.0	-2.1	5.5
Waltaine Income Fund	2.8	8.3	–	–	–	–	–	–	–	–
HIGHEST IN GROUP	13.2	16.1	21.2	41.3	10.9	50.8	19.4	8.2	13.3	16.6
LOWEST IN GROUP	-3.2	2.9	6.1	11.0	-6.0	10.7	-4.9	-14.1	-5.0	4.6
AVERAGE OF GROUP	7.4	7.9	14.3	24.3	3.4	30.6	13.0	-1.4	5.0	7.7

Fund	1988	1987	1986	1985	1984	1983	1982	1981	1980	1979
PREFERRED DIVIDEND FUNDS										
AGF Preferred Income Fund	3.6	7.6	10.2	–	–	–	–	–	–	–
AMD Dividend Fund	1.5	6.2	8.6	–	–	–	–	–	–	–
Allied Dividend Fund	0.5	5.5	–	–	–	–	–	–	–	–
Bolton Tremblay Income Fund	3.1	9.7	7.7	13.4	4.4	30.2	14.3	-0.4	9.8	7.3
Bullock Dividend Fund	0.0	6.2	10.7	–	–	–	–	–	–	–
Dynamic Dividend Fund	5.9	11.1	–	–	–	–	–	–	–	–
Guardian Pfd Dividend Fund	3.9	8.7	–	–	–	–	–	–	–	–
Investors Dividend Fund	3.6	9.9	9.8	24.2	2.5	55.3	-14.9	6.6	4.5	27.5
Montreal Trust Dividend Fund	-4.7	–	–	–	–	–	–	–	–	–
Morgan Dividend Fund	-3.9	12.0	–	–	–	–	–	–	–	–
Mutual Dividend Fund	3.7	8.6	–	–	–	–	–	–	–	–
PH&N Dividend Income Fund	2.0	18.8	10.2	20.3	0.8	56.7	-11.1	9.5	6.5	19.7
Prudential Dividend Fund	6.4	–	–	–	–	–	–	–	–	–
Royal Trust Preferred Fund	0.7	7.2	–	–	–	–	–	–	–	–
Spectrum Dividend Fund	3.4	–	–	–	–	–	–	–	–	–
Viking Dividend Fund Ltd	3.5	11.5	15.3	23.5	6.2	55.4	-14.3	9.2	5.2	–
Waltaine Conv Preferred Fund	-5.0	13.6	–	–	–	–	–	–	–	–
HIGHEST IN GROUP	6.4	18.8	15.3	24.2	6.2	56.7	14.3	9.5	9.8	27.5
LOWEST IN GROUP	-5.0	5.5	7.7	13.4	0.8	30.2	-14.9	-0.4	4.5	7.3
AVERAGE OF GROUP	1.7	9.8	10.4	20.4	3.5	49.4	-6.5	6.2	6.5	18.2
MONEY MARKET FUNDS										
AGF Money Market Fund	8.4	7.8	9.2	10.8	9.4	12.0	18.2	14.7	13.6	9.7
AMD Money Market Fd	8.3	7.9	9.6	–	–	–	–	–	–	–
AMD US Dollar Money Mkt(US$)	6.2	–	–	–	–	–	–	–	–	–
Allied Money Fund	8.1	7.9	–	–	–	–	–	–	–	–
Bolton Tremblay Money Fund	8.7	8.2	9.4	11.0	9.1	11.6	–	–	–	–
CDA Money Market Fund	8.2	7.5	9.6	11.0	9.5	11.5	16.1	14.1	11.6	8.2
CMA Short-Term Deposit Fund	7.6	7.1	9.0	10.5	9.3	11.6	17.5	13.3	13.5	10.1
Cda Life Money Market S-29	7.3	6.0	7.7	10.0	9.3	12.4	17.2	14.7	12.3	9.1
Cdn Gen Life Ins Money Mkt C	7.2	–	–	–	–	–	–	–	–	–
Crown Life Pen Short Term	9.3	7.4	10.0	10.8	9.0	11.3	17.1	–	–	–
Dynamic Money Market Fund	8.0	7.2	8.9	10.3	–	–	–	–	–	–
Elliott & Page Money Fund	9.4	9.1	10.6	–	–	–	–	–	–	–
Everest Short Term Asset Fd	7.8	–	–	–	–	–	–	–	–	–
Ficadre Monetaire	7.0	7.5	8.9	–	–	–	–	–	–	–
Guardian Short Term Money Fund	8.7	7.7	9.3	10.7	9.3	11.4	17.7	13.9	9.6	9.8
Industrial Cash Management Fd	8.1	7.8	9.5	–	–	–	–	–	–	–
Investors Money Market Fund	8.3	7.2	8.9	–	–	–	–	–	–	–
MER Money Market Fund	4.0	6.7	9.0	10.6	7.8	–	–	–	–	–
MONY T-Bill Fund	6.9	–	–	–	–	–	–	–	–	–
Mutual Money Market Fund	7.7	6.2	8.6	–	–	–	–	–	–	–
Ordre Ingenieurs Revenu Var	8.1	8.4	9.3	11.6	9.3	14.3	17.0	13.2	11.2	9.2
PH&N Money Market Fund	8.3	–	–	–	–	–	–	–	–	–
Prudential Money Market Fund	8.8	–	–	–	–	–	–	–	–	–
RoyFund Money Market Fd	7.8	–	–	–	–	–	–	–	–	–
Sentinel Cda Money Market Fd	9.7	–	–	–	–	–	–	–	–	–
Spectrum Cash Reserve Fund	8.0	–	–	–	–	–	–	–	–	–

Fund	1988	1987	1986	1985	1984	1983	1982	1981	1979	1978
St-Laurent Reer-Epargne-Plus	8.3	9.0	–	–	–	–	–	–	–	–
Talvest Money Fund	9.5	4.9	–	–	–	–	–	–	–	–
Trimark Interest Fund	8.6	–	–	–	–	–	–	–	–	–
HIGHEST IN GROUP	11.2	9.1	10.6	11.6	9.5	14.3	18.2	14.7	13.6	10.1
LOWEST IN GROUP	4.0	4.9	7.7	10.0	7.8	11.3	16.1	13.2	9.6	8.2
AVERAGE OF GROUP	8.1	7.5	9.3	10.7	9.1	12.0	17.3	14.0	12.0	9.4
MARKET INDICES										
91 Day Canada T Bill	8.7	8.0	9.3	10.7	10.0	10.7	16.5	14.8	12.9	10.2
Consumer Price Index	4.1	4.6	4.1	4.0	4.8	5.4	11.8	12.3	9.4	9.3
MYW Weighted 50 Mid-Term Index	8.6	7.7	17.2	34.0	-1.1	41.8	10.5	-6.1	–	–
Standard & Poor's 500 Index	-15.3	20.6	38.2	34.9	2.2	53.3	-5.0	26.0	15.4	18.4
TSE Total Return Index	-5.2	24.6	17.4	26.6	-6.1	86.6	-39.1	18.8	32.6	49.9